NAPLES & THE AMALFI COAST

BY
RYAN LEVITT

Produced by
Thomas Cook Publishing

Written by Ryan Levitt

Original photography by Conor Caffrey
Original design by Laburnum Technologies
Pvt Ltd

Editing and page layout by Cambridge
Publishing Management Limited,
149B Histon Road, Cambridge CB4 3JD

Published by Thomas Cook Publishing
A division of Thomas Cook Tour Operations Limited

PO Box 227, The Thomas Cook Business Park, Unit 15/16,
Coningsby Road, Peterborough PE3 8SB, United Kingdom
E-mail: books@thomascook.com
www.thomascookpublishing.com

ISBN: 1-841573-89-2

Text © 2004 Thomas Cook Publishing
Maps © 2004 Thomas Cook Publishing
First edition © 2004 Thomas Cook Publishing

Head of Thomas Cook Publishing: Donald Greig
Project Editor: Charlotte Christensen
Project Administration: Michelle Warrington
DTP: Steven Collins

Printed and bound in Spain by: Grafo Industrias Gráficas, Basauri

Cover: Town view of Positano. Photograph by zefa visual media ltd
Inside cover: All photos by Brand X Pictures/Alamy, except bottom left by
ImageGap/Alamy

CD manufacturing services provided by business interactive ltd, Rutland, UK.
CD edited and designed by Laburnum Technologies Pvt Ltd

KU-498-735

Contents

Introduction

Conquered throughout the ages by numerous counts and courts, the city of Naples combines influences from dozens of regions across the European continent. Spanish architecture, Baroque splendour, Italian flair and the Arabian kasbah come together in this city overlooked and often overshadowed by Mount Vesuvius – the volcano that gives the region both its incredibly fertile soil and its somewhat threatening reputation.

The Neapolitan spirit is one that Anglo-Saxons often find difficult to comprehend. Whether arriving by plane, train or boat, the sight of Naples' choking traffic, crumbling masonry and the frequent arm-flailing and dramatic street-side arguments amongst its charismatic citizens may make you wonder why you ever decided to book a

From yesterday ...

holiday here. Don't take this fear of the foreign as a sign to flee to Capri, Ischia or any of the more salubrious locales dotted in and around the Bay of Naples – rather, take the time to scratch the dusty and garbage-strewn streets to discover this city brimming with culture, incredible gourmet delights, secret palazzo hideaways, labyrinthine alleyways and a sense of excitement unsurpassed anywhere else in Italy.

This chaotic atmosphere owes much to the area's survival sense. Naples has faced destruction in the eye on more than just a few occasions, whether it be due to wartime bombings, aching poverty or natural disasters. But its future is looking up. A Neapolitan revival has been brewing for the past decade or so, ever since the city hosted the G7 meeting of economic superpowers back in 1994. As part of the clean-up campaign tied in with the city's summit duties, new metro stations were built, the national *Mani Pulite* (clean hands) campaign was launched to reduce corruption, and city streets and roadways were brightened up to showcase the city and its Renaissance to the world. Poverty and crime may still exist, but the likelihood of foreigners being on the receiving end of theft and muggings is exceedingly slim – as long as you don't go around flashing your new Rolex to the masses.

While the city continues to be one of the most cash-strapped in the nation, it can still put on a really good show. Opera performances at Teatro San Carlo – Italy's oldest theatre – are reputed to be second only to Milan's La Scala.

The art collections at the Museo di Capodimonte are packed with examples of the masters from the 17th to the 19th centuries, and the treasures of Pompeii are brilliantly illuminated in the massive Museo Nazionale Archeologico. If you time it right, you may even be able to catch one of the temporary exhibitions of cutting-edge modern art at the Castel Sant'Elmo. And that's not even including the painstakingly excavated ruins of Pompeii and Herculaneum, the trappings of the island playgrounds of the rich – Capri and Ischia – or the jaw-dropping views and cliff-side towns that dot the Amalfi Coast.

So pour yourself a glass of *limoncello*, find yourself a cosy view of the bay and prepare yourself for an unforgettable experience enjoyed by millions of tourists since the days when a few ancient Greek explorers decided that this corner of the Med would make a nice place to live. You may be branded a *straniero* (foreigner), but you're sure to be given a welcome that will make you feel right at home.

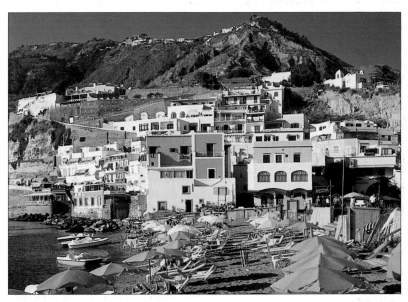

… to today

The City

At 40.8 degrees North, 14.4 degrees East, the city of Naples is the third largest city in Italy (after Milan and Rome), and is situated directly on the Bay of Naples, which stretches from the port town of Pozzuoli in the north to the sweeping Sorrento Peninsula in the south. Just over 40km (25 miles) separates the two corners of the bay as the crow flies. Naples is approximately one third of the way down the coastline from Pozzuoli on the way to Sorrento and the Amalfi Coast.

Piazza dei Martiri

Naples proper boasts a population of just over 1¼ million. Including the suburbs, this number increases to 3 million inhabitants dwelling in geographic locations as diverse as the fertile Campania plain and the high grounds, craters and hills formed by ancient volcanoes. Most of the commutable population is linked by train services that plod their way alongside the Bay of Naples coastline at frequent intervals throughout the day.

The islands of Capri, Ischia and Procida are located just off the Campanian coast. Ferries link the islands to each other and to the port towns of Pozzuoli, Sorrento, Stabia, Positano and Naples. Ferry rides between the islands and Naples take approximately an hour and fifteen minutes. Less time is required if you catch one of the frequent rapid hydrofoils.

Climate

Naples boasts a Mediterranean climate that ranges in heat from up to 40°C (105°F) in the height of summer down to 0°C (32°F) in December and January. During the peak months of July and August, temperatures in the city can be sweltering with extremely high humidity levels doing little to alleviate the heat. The islands of Capri, Ischia and Procida experience cooling sea breezes during this period, yet also become packed with tourists, thus making any climatic benefits minimal when combined with the volume of humanity flocking to their sun-kissed shores.

Spring and autumn are often the best times to visit, when limited tourist numbers and invariably warm temperatures show Naples at its best. Hotel bookings tend to be down during this shoulder season, which often affords optimum weather conditions and better options for a tight budget. March, April and September occasionally experience heavy showers, but they quickly disappear to leave the city bathed in crystal-clear air and cleaner, washed-down streets. The post-shower period is the perfect time to search for higher ground and capture city panoramas when Naples is bathed in a golden glow.

Between November and February, the air becomes clear and cold, rarely dropping below freezing. The winter months often dust snow on the top of Vesuvius, giving it an alpine resort look. While you run the risk of dreary, wet weather during the colder months, the periods of drizzle and cloud invariably leave within a couple of days to reveal spectacularly clear views.

The areas of Naples

The geography of the city is largely determined by the hills and coastline carved by the ancient volcanic activity of the area. While the Centro Storico is the heart of Naples, it is by no means the only district worth exploring. The oldest part of the city, its streets are maze-like, twisting and turning according to the needs of merchants and residents of times gone by. Disasters, destruction and subsequent unregulated rebuilding have done much to complete the seemingly chaotic mess of Neapolitan traffic. The ancient Greeks attempted to impose order on the place with a grid pattern of streets in central Naples, but development throughout the ages has largely obliterated this original attempt at order. The Port and University district is predominantly an industrial wasteland. Attempts are being made to clean up the area in order to revitalise the community and remove a few of the more distracting and polluting sights, but the bureaucracy and poverty of the city has made project development slow to come to fruition. This area lies due

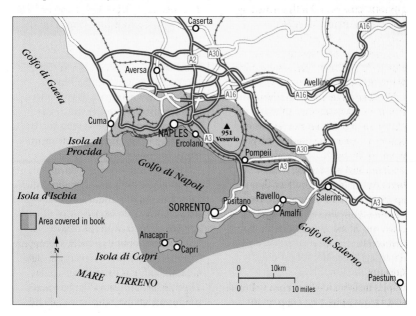

Mornings on the Med – Naples Port

south of the Centro Storico directly on the waters of the Bay of Naples. The Via Duomo bisects both neighbourhoods almost directly down the middle and acts as a convenient road to traverse between the two communities.

Royal Naples, situated west of the main port, holds the bulk of the treasures of Naples' regal past, including the Palazzo Reale and the Castel dell'Ovo. Noted more for its shopping and archaeological treasures is the Quartieri Spagnole, almost directly north of the Royal Naples quarter. To reach the Quartieri Spagnole, follow the sound of ringing cash registers up

the Via Toledo towards the Museo Nazionale Archeologico. If you enter Sanità (anywhere east of the Archaeological Museum) then you've gone too far. The lack of department stores should be your first clue.

Two hills sandwich the city against the port – Vomero and Capodimonte. Both are relatively middle-class neighbourhoods with a bevy of attractions to draw in the masses. Luxury hotel options line the Corso Vittorio Emanuele in Vomero, with the Castel Sant'Elmo providing excellent views of the city below. Vomero is also where you will find the funiculars the city is famous for. Via Scarlatti acts as the centre of Vomero, with the Piazza Vanvitelli at its heart.

Difficult to get to, Capodimonte is largely residential. Other than the Museo di Capodimonte, there should be no reason to warrant a visit. Exercise fanatics may want to check out the grounds around the museum – local joggers flock to the gardens for its clear air and lush greenery. Capodimonte is situated north of the Centro Storico.

Finally, for lovers of high fashion and even higher prices, Chiaia is the place to go. Located further west along the coast from the Port district, the streets around the Riviera di Chiaia – especially tiny Via Calabritto – hold exclusive Italian designer wear and interiors boutiques. The stroll along the Via Francesco Caracciolo towards Mergellina is especially loved by natives during the summer months due to the cooling breezes of the Mediterranean that kiss the gardens lining the coast along this route.

Those looking to get out of town should note that boats and hydrofoils bound for Procida, Ischia and Capri depart from the Molo Beverello in the Port district, while the Circumvesuviana trains towards Pompeii, Herculaneum and the Amalfi Coast leave from the Stazione Circumvesuviana and not the Stazione Centrale. The Stazione Circumvesuviana is located on the southern edge of the Port and University neighbourhood.

Parked in the Piazza Dante

History

8th century BC	The Greeks arrive in Ischia, establishing a colony at Cuma.
470 BC	Neapolis is founded by the Greeks.
326 BC	Romans conquer Neapolis, bringing the Roman Empire to the region.
100 BC – AD 100	Campania becomes the playground of the rich of the Roman Empire.
AD 27–37	Emperor Tiberius arrives in Capri and decides to stay. The Roman Empire's seat of power is moved to the island.
AD 79	The eruption of Vesuvius destroys Pompeii and Herculaneum.
5th century	Goths and Vandals take sporadic control of the city, leaving desecration and destruction in their wake.
536	The Byzantine Emperor Justinian captures the city.
581, 592 and 599	Lombards and Saracens lay siege to Naples – the invaders are defeated each time.
645	Basilio becomes the first native Duke of Neapolis, and the city flourishes under his rule.
1062–1077	The Normans take Capua, Amalfi and Salerno.
1130	Roger II – a Norman – is crowned King of Sicily.
1139	Neapolitans swear allegiance to the Sicilian crown. Naples falls into decline as power and revenue travel to Palermo. The city's population is 30,000.
1194	The end of the Norman line. Tancred, last Norman ruler of Naples, dies. Henry of Swabia, the son of the Holy Roman Emperor, takes control. He becomes King Henry I of Sicily.

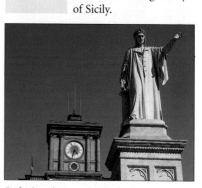

Go forth and conquer – Charles III

Garibaldi – a unifying influence

1214	Frederick II becomes King of Southern Italy and Holy Roman Emperor upon the death of his father Henry I. Under his leadership, a university is founded in 1224.
1251	The death of Frederick II divides the city as Naples declares itself a free commune. The Imperial forces of German King Conrad (son of Frederick) win back the city in 1253.
1256	Sicily is taken by Charles of Anjou, beginning a brief period of French reign. The capital is moved from Palermo back to Naples.
1302	Sicily is given by Charles of Anjou to the Aragonese.
1442	Alfonso of Aragon takes control of Sicily. Southern Italy is unified once again.
1494	France's King Charles VIII occupies the city on the invitation of the noble classes. The Neapolitan people rebel and reinstate the Aragonese King, Ferdinand II.
1502	The first of the hated Spanish viceroys rules the city as Ferdinand III leaves. Viceroys continue to rule over Naples for the next 250 years.
1600	Naples, with its population of 300,000, becomes Europe's largest city.
1606	Caravaggio arrives in Naples. His influence on local art is enormous.
1631	Vesuvius erupts and 3,500 are killed.
1647	Local stallholder and fisherman Masaniello declares revolution in the city, protesting against crippling Spanish taxes. Nine days later he is assassinated, yet revolts continue across the region.
1656	Plague kills three-quarters of the population, and the local economy is devastated. The Baroque period begins, as survivors attempt to replace the everyday with the ornate.

Naples' Duomo

1707	Naples is occupied by Austria. Viceroys continue to rule for the next 27 years.
1734	Charles Bourbon, son of Philip V of Spain, expels the Austrians and becomes Charles III of Sicily. Naples is reinstated as the capital.
1737	Teatro San Carlo, Italy's oldest theatre, is built.
1748	The excavations of Pompeii and Herculaneum commence.
1757	King Charles abdicates to succeed his father as King of Spain.
1768	Ferdinand, son of Charles, marries Maria Carolina – the daughter of the Austrian empress. By 1777, she ousts all reformers and backs the leadership of Briton Sir John Acton. Acton eventually takes over running the kingdom in all but name.
1798	Rome is taken from the French by the Neapolitans – for exactly 11 days.
1799	The royal family flees on Nelson's ship to Sicily after invasion by the French. Intellectuals back a republic, while working classes remain staunchly royal. Ferdinand returns following defeat of the republicans. Two hundred rebels are executed.
1806	France takes Naples again – this time under the leadership of Joseph Bonaparte. Royals escape to Sicily.
1816	Royals return to Naples and Ferdinand resumes his rule.
1820	Uprising by the Carbonari group forces Ferdinand to grant a constitution.
1821	Austrian troops invade on the invitation of Ferdinand in order to quash constitutional government.
1848	Naples' parliament demands a constitution. A year later, Ferdinand's son dissolves government.
1860	Naples joins the United Kingdom of Italy after Garibaldi and the

	unification troops enter the city.
1884	Serious cholera outbreak forces the city to examine infrastructure and housing issues.
1880–1914	Two and a half million Italians – mostly from the south – emigrate to North America.
1943	Allied bombs destroy Naples. Citizens liberate the city in the *Quattro giornate napoletane*. Germans ruin infrastructure as they flee the city.
1943–9	One third of Neapolitan women are forced into prostitution. The *camorra* (mafia) and black market begin their reign of terror.
1944	Vesuvius erupts, killing 26.
1946	National referendum ousts the Italian monarchy against the wishes of the Neapolitan public. Vittorio Emanuele sails from Naples, as local son Enrico de Nicola is voted in as the first president of the Italian republic.
1950–93	The Christian Democrat party rules the city. Many

	candidates are backed by the powerful *camorra* clans. Unregulated development and industrialisation transform the city.
1971	A government report finds that most postwar buildings are both illegal and unsafe.
1973	Cholera hits the city again.
1980	Three thousand are killed and thousands left homeless when an earthquake rocks the city.
1992	*Mani Pulite* (clean hands) anti-corruption campaign is launched.
1993	Left-winger Antonio Bassolino is elected mayor. Neapolitan Renaissance is launched.
1994	The G7 summit is held in the city.
2001	The Global Forum is held in Naples. Anti-globalisation riots rock the city protesting against the meeting. Over 100 are injured.
2002	Eight police are arrested following an inquiry into the Global Forum riots. New metro stations open.

Governance

The Italian Republic was formed in 1946 following the banishment of Vittorio Emanuele (son of Italy's last king, Umberto II). Over 50 governments have been elected since the first one under the leadership of Naples-born Enrico de Nicola.

The Fascist era

The Government

The country is governed by a parliamentary system (*Parlamento*), based in the Italian capital of Rome, and consisting of a Senate (*Senato della Republica*) and the Chamber of Deputies (*Camera dei Deputati*). The executive branch is made up of an elected chief of state – currently President Carlo Azeglio. The President appoints a Prime Minister and confirms the appointment with the parliament. Right-wing media baron Silvio Berlusconi currently holds the post.

The head of state is the President, who is elected by an electoral college consisting of both Houses of Parliament

An Italian icon

and 58 regional representatives. The Prime Minister acts as the head of government, referred to in Italy as President of the Council of Ministers. The Council of Ministers acts as the Italian cabinet, with posts being appointed by the Prime Minister and approved by the President. A five-party government alliance consisting of the Forza Italia, National Alliance, Northern League, Democratic Christian Centre and United Christian Democrats currently controls power.

There are 315 seats in the Houses of Parliament, of which 232 are directly elected and 83 elected by regional proportional representation. Seats are held for a term of five years. A limited number of members-for-life, including former presidents of the Republic, also hold seats. The 630 members of the senate serve five-year terms, of which 475 are directly elected, with 155 by proportional representation.

The republic is divided into 20 regions or counties. Naples is the administrative capital of the county of Campania. The surrounding areas of Amalfi, Ischia, Capri, and the ruins of Pompeii and Herculaneum, are also within Campania's borders.

Local government

For 50 years following the end of World War II, Naples was controlled by the Christian Democrats who were backed by the economic and political might of the crime-fuelled *camorra* clans. Most of Naples' crumbling postwar architecture can be attributed to the unregulated and illegal construction undertaken by mafia-controlled developers. Local leaders and police forces turned a blind eye, until the earthquake of 1980 destroyed acres of property due to the poor building codes and practices maintained by shady construction companies.

Between 1983 and 1993, ten mayors succeeded each other during the post-quake chaos. During this problematic decade, public services ground to a halt. Only 300 buses served a population of over 2 million, and rubbish collection was left to constantly-striking *camorra*-backed conglomerates.

The national 'clean hands' campaign – launched in 1993 – provided the impetus needed to bring about the dawn of a new Neapolitan Renaissance. Communist Antonio Bassolino was voted in as mayor, narrowly defeating the campaign of Alessandra Mussolini, granddaughter of the wartime leader. Under Bassolino's control, the city enjoyed a massive clean-up, restoring the Centro Storico in time for the 1994 G7 summit meeting. After gaining re-election in 1997, Bassolino lost much of his popular support as cracks amongst his fractured coalition of aligned parties began to show. Naples' first female mayor, Rosa Russo Jervolino, stepped into city hall in 2000. Unfortunately, she too is hampered by a coalition government who spend more time arguing amongst themselves than they do in passing public policies and developing projects.

A city of rebellion

Many cities have experienced periods of tragedy – yet few have come back from the number of disasters and volume of destruction thrust upon the poor citizens of Naples. Lava, disease and earthquakes have all attempted to flatten the city at some point during its history, yet locals keep coming back for more.

Thar' she blows

Until the deadly blast of AD 79, travellers, merchants and farmers visiting the Campanian coastline were drawn to the area because of its unusually fertile soil. While farmers realised that the nutrient-rich earth owed its value to the volcanic activity of Vesuvius, few could have seen that the price tag in lives

attached to this rural splendour would cost so much. Even after the devastation of 79, little was done to prevent future calamities – the natural beauty, fabulous farmland and convenient ports made sure residents would choose to stick it out rather than give up their precious homelands.

But volcanoes and red-hot lava aren't the only things that have threatened Naples during its 2,400-year history. At various times, Naples has been decimated by plague, cholera, earthquake, bombings, war and famine. Modern-day Neapolitans have yet to learn the lessons of the past, as a number of local deaths can be attributed to shoddy postwar construction practices that resulted in the collapse of thousands of buildings and continued crumbling masonry following the 'quake of 1980.

Unlike future-thinking, earthquake-prone nations like Japan, Italy – specifically the city of Naples – does little to ensure that buildings don't collapse during an earth tremor. While the laws are in place, the mafia constantly flouts them. Until 1993, local newspaper headlines reported on construction scandals on an almost daily basis. Winning a seat in the Campanian government was like writing yourself a blank cheque, as long as you worked together with the *camorra* clans and didn't get caught by a periodic police raid or investigative journalist.

Above: Volcanic rock on Vesuvius
Left: Victims of the disaster at Pompeii

Chaos reigns

The threat of daily destruction is reflected in the way Neapolitans choose to live their lives. Traffic chaos rules supreme, business appointments are often minutes, if not hours later than they are scheduled for, a lunch could take you well into the late hours of the evening and building developments go up higgledy-piggledy on every corner of land possible. Of course, this lifestyle choice often results in even more destruction and calamity, but you might as well be surrounded by splendid Baroque architecture, rather than a soulless, yet earthquake-proof, high-rise.

CENTRO DIREZIONALE

As the rest of the world profited from the 'greed is good' era of the 1980s, Naples fell into a state of serious decline. Desperate to attract big business, the local government launched the city's largest ever publicly managed construction project – the Centro Direzionale. Designed by Japanese architect Kenzo Tange, the Centro Direzionale is comprised of a series of ultramodern skyscrapers with an emphasis on the glass and concrete popular during the flashy 1980s. Situated on a stretch of isolated, marshy land cleared by the bombs of World War II, the project never really took off as the anticipated injection of capital failed to materialise. Delays, bribery and scandal continue to plague the project, remaining far from completion to this day.

Culture and Festivals

The citizens of Naples are of the 'work-to-live' mindset, revelling in the parties, festivals and religious occasions that bring a halt to major sections of the city on a daily basis. You won't need to give a Neapolitan too many excuses to kick off early for the day – especially when faced with the typically glorious weather and crystal-clear panoramas that characterise the surrounding countryside.

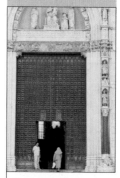
Duomo entrance

Religion

Neapolitans would like to think that religion continues to play an important part of everyday life, and in many ways it does – for the older generations, at least. As the geographic home of the Roman Catholic Church, many local customs and laws acknowledge church doctrine, yet embrace the modern requirements of western society.

Due to the disasters that continually befall the city, Neapolitan Christianity has evolved into a mish-mash of ancient superstition, belief in miraculous occurrences and cultish behaviour. Many believers continue to pray to the skulls of the deceased, and the bulk of the population still adheres to the prophecies that revolve around the annual liquefaction of the blood of

The stunning interior of the Teatro di San Carlo

Religion is an important part of Neapolitan life

San Gennaro. If San Gennaro's blood doesn't start flowing then it might as well be raining toads from the heavens. Everything from a Napoli football team loss to nuclear war will be blamed on the fact that the annual miracle failed to transpire.

Body language

Neapolitans are famous for their body language. In a culture as macho as this one, most of the arm flailing, finger pointing and wailing you spot will probably be more for show than anything else. Most arguments you see

will be a result of traffic accidents – more common than you might think. So if you find that you experience a fender-bender, the best course of action is to apologise profusely while the other driver lets off a bit of steam, even if the crash isn't your fault.

Surprisingly, English is not commonly spoken by locals. You will find that tourist traps, popular restaurants, shops and hotels will understand the basics, but when it comes down to the nitty-gritty of directions and information, you'll be left to your own devices.

Nightlife

If you're planning a night out on the town, you might want to catch some sleep during the evening. Most nights don't get going until the wee hours of the morning. Nightclubs and cafés may be open throughout the evening, but you'll find them empty and lacking in atmosphere until at least midnight. Early dinners are unheard of in this town. In many cases you will find restaurants locked tight during the hours when you traditionally enjoy your last meal of the day.

One of the nicest things to do is to take a simple stroll along the seaside or through the Centro Storico at night. While the streets aren't well lit, you'll find plenty of other couples enjoying the night air.

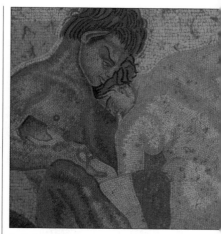

Erotic Roman art

MATCH-DAY MADNESS

Footie has been taking over the hearts and minds of Neapolitans since 1905 when the crew of an English cargo ship challenged a team of local dignitaries to a match. The British connection remained throughout Napoli's early love affair with the sport right up until 1926 when local team Napoli SSC was founded under the direction of their first manager, Englishman Willy Garbutt.

If you're a fan of footie, then there's no better place to watch a match than from the grandstands of Stadio San Paolo. While tickets on match day are like gold dust, there are always plenty of touts hanging around outside the stadium to part you from your hard-earned cash.

Major festivals

The two major festivals celebrated in Naples are Christmas and the feast of the city's patron saint, San Gennaro, held on 19 September.

Christmas is a beautiful time to visit the city. Shopping reaches an almost frenzied pace in the streets around San Gregorio Armeno where locals stock up on figures for their traditional Nativity scenes. Almost every church in town has a Christmas crib, the finest being in the Palazzo Reale and in San Martino.

The feast of San Gennaro, while less important religiously to the world at large, literally controls and foretells the fortunes of the two million people who call Naples home. According to tradition, the blood of San Gennaro is supposed to liquefy on 19 September every year to honour his day as patron saint of the city. Frantic praying continues throughout the day at the *Duomo*, as black-clad devotees cluster around the gory artefact. Tradition says that if the blood fails to liquefy, then the upcoming year is sure to be a bad one.

Footie fanatics

While not strictly a holiday, you will find that the city screeches to a halt whenever the local football team, Napoli SSC, has a match. While far from the glory days of the late 1980s when Argentinean superstar Maradona led the team to its first ever *scudetto* (league title), the Stadio San Paolo still manages to pull in fans. Ensure a healthy state of mind on match days by remaining as far away as possible from the western suburbs, where the stadium is located.

Stadio San Paolo

Quiet conservatism

Italian morals are decidedly anachronistic, especially in the south. While the north votes conservative and thinks liberally, Napoli and the surrounding countryside vote communist and think conservatively.

Religious icons are everywhere

Much of this attitude is due to the strong influence that the Roman Catholic Church holds on residents of the area. Neapolitans are generally tolerant towards racial, religious and sexual minorities, choosing to ignore any obvious displays of 'individuality' rather than express any formal disdain.

Hearth and home

Chivalry remains alive and well in Naples. This is a town where young men still get up out of their seats on public transit for the benefit of a woman of any age. At the heart of Neapolitan life is the family. If a local has made plans weeks in advance and their grandmother calls them for lunch, then they will cancel everything to see their beloved nana. Respect for elders remains strong, so if you exhibit the slightest sign of a wrinkle, you'll find Neapolitan youth extremely accommodating.

Children are especially loved by one and all. Prepare your son or daughter – if you are bringing them along – for much cheek-pinching, cooing and general admiration. Complete strangers love to dote over a baby, with some holding packages of sweets just for the purpose of giving them to your cherubic child.

Certosa-Museo di San Martino

Café society at the Gambrinus

Impressions

Naples is quite a broad city, squished lengthways along the Bay of Naples by the hills of Capodimonte, Vomero and Vesuvius. Walking around neighbourhoods is extremely easy, but distances between varying districts can be a bit of a trek. The city is neither pedestrian nor traffic-friendly. A new, extensive metro system is doing a little to alleviate the legendary traffic jams that cripple the city centre, but there are still vast areas that aren't served by the new subway lines.

Perfect panorama

City layout

Other than the winding streets of the Centro Storico and the distinctive hills of Capodimonte and Vomero, Neapolitan neighbourhoods aren't all that well-defined – at least not in the eyes of the average tourist. Residents of Chiaia, with their seaside views and exclusive boutiques, tend to be slightly snobbier than those who dwell in the industrial wastelands of the Port and University. Meanwhile, the citizens of Toledo and Sanità are overwhelmingly close-knit.

Plans to modernise the beleaguered Port and University district have been underway for years. If the project ever gets off the ground – and the volume of bickering at City Hall is doing much to prevent this – then entire tracts of disused factories and industrial wasteland will be cleared to allow locals the possibility of reclaiming the Bay of Naples.

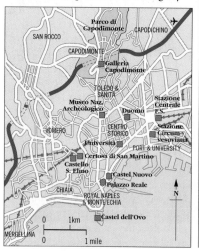

When to go

Peak season in Naples is during the summer. Crowds pack the city streets and temperatures soar. High humidity blankets the area, with sea breezes doing little to combat the sweaty and stifling surroundings. Savvy locals get out of town as fast as possible during the months of July and August, doing as the tourists do by flocking to the Amalfi

Ancient alleys in Castel Oro

Coast and the islands of Capri and Ischia.

Spring and autumn are invariably pleasant. Temperatures rarely drop much below 20°C (70°F) and occasional rainstorms leave the city and the views from Vomero crystal clear. The offshore islands are best in March and October: the crowds will be gone and there may be fewer hotel and restaurant options, but there is often a good chance of experiencing freak summer-like weather.

From November to February, temperatures drop, sometimes to almost 0°C (32°F). A light dusting of snow can often be spotted on the top of Vesuvius and the air is clear and sweet. Occasional periods of grey, dreary weather hit the city during this period, only to leave a few days later.

Getting around

Until the new metro system is completed, visitors will have to rely on the power of their two feet and their taxi-hailing hands. While the city is relatively compact, it does stretch quite a bit along the Bay of Naples, making a full day of walking an exhausting prospect.

Taxis can be found at ranks dotted throughout the city. While inexpensive compared to the fares of other major cities, drivers are notorious for their scams. Make sure to insist that the meter is turned on before you depart or you'll be ripped off at the end of your journey.

Buses are plentiful in Naples, with almost all the lines running from the bus depot outside the Piazza Garibaldi. Give yourself lots of time using this option, however, as the buses stop at almost every corner in the city and their large size makes navigation through the minute city streets extremely difficult.

For longer distances, trains and ferries are the way to go. With Capri, Procida and Ischia you have no other option than to use the boats that leave the mainland on an almost hourly basis.

Go underground to get around

Long-distance train services to Rome and the other major centres of Italy arrive and depart from Stazione Centrale in Piazza Garibaldi. Journeys along the Campania coastline to Pompeii, Herculaneum, Amalfi and Sorrento, depart from the Stazione Circumvesuviana on Corso Garibaldi. Trains run regularly throughout the day until about midnight.

Driving in the city

Driving in Naples is legendarily awful. Tiny streets, crumbling asphalt, constant repaving and a high reliance on automobiles as a form of transport combine to transform the city into one of the world's biggest parking lots. If you do decide to drive, you'll be doing so in a city where drivers constantly flout laws – often in a most dangerous manner.

In the summer, the streets of Ischia, Procida, Sorrento and the Amalfi Coast are absolutely jammed, especially at weekends. If you must bring your car, make sure to do so on weekdays only. On many Sundays vehicular traffic is banned. Check with your concierge or car rental agency to confirm dates.

Pollution and litter

If you're used to clean streets and tree-lined avenues, then you may be in for a shock. The streets of Naples can sometimes resemble a refuse dump. The paralysing traffic does little to help the situation, with air pollution rising to levels that asthmatics may find difficult to deal with. When everything becomes a bit too untidy for comfort, flee to the more subdued neighbourhoods of

Vomero or Capodimonte. The hillside perches of these two districts provide a release from the smog, and large open spaces to enjoy a rarefied country air.

Manners and mores

Neapolitans are a blunt, relaxed, in-your-face and excitable people. If you meet a local in the street, don't be surprised if they give you a hug or pecks on the cheek. Same-sex hand-holding on the street is not a sign of homosexuality in Naples, merely one of affection. Personal space areas are much smaller in Naples than you may be used to at home. If excited, Neapolitans will gesticulate wildly, using body language to emphasise their point.

If you are going out on the town, plan for a long evening. Waiters are of the continental variety and will do as little as possible to present you with something as annoying as a bill. Meals are an event and are intended to be savoured. If in a rush, you will have to emphasise this fact to the staff as often as possible. And whatever you do, don't get mad or the staff will go out of their way to get even. In Naples, the customer is always wrong.

The cost of living

Italy has a reputation for being an expensive place to visit. Naples and the rest of the South are relatively affordable, as they are situated in the southern, and consequently less wealthy, half of the country. The exception to this rule occurs in the resort and heavily-touristed areas of Capri, Ischia and the Amalfi Coast where prices go up, up and away.

Architecture

The history of Naples stretches as far back as the days of the Greek Empire, and so does its architecture. Once Europe's most populous city, residents have slept in grottoes, alleyways, warehouses and churchyards at any given period, depending upon their place in society. Its rapidly reproducing citizenry meant architects needed to design residences that built up rather than out. Look up when you walk through the streets to see the results.

Bay of Naples

The Greek influence

Remnants of Greek architecture are difficult to find within greater Naples. For glimpses of Ancient Athenian rule, you'll have to go into the Campanian countryside to the temples of Paestum and Cuma. Little remains from the days when a prosperous settlement known as Paleopolis covered the area, but its influences remain.

The Roman Age

Romans followed many of the original Greek plans, especially their main roads and intersections. Piazza Bellini, while a hub of activity and life today, originally marked the edge of Greek city limits – the original city walls can be found a metre under the ground at this point.

Two of the most important churches in the city lie directly above important hubs of Roman life. Located under the Duomo and the church of San Lorenzo Maggiore are artefacts from Roman market life, while the original Roman baths have been included in a museum built behind the church of Santa Chiara.

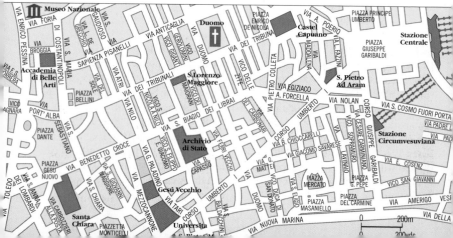

For the best examples of Roman architecture, you should make the trip to Pompeii and Herculaneum. These preserved towns, destroyed during the eruption of Vesuvius in AD 79 should tell you everything you will probably ever want to know about the period – and more.

From the Normans to the Baroque

After the Normans named Naples as the capital of Sicily in the 11th century, a flurry of building activity was set in motion. Castel dell'Ovo and Castel Capuano were built to provide homes and fortifications for the leaders of the kingdom, while city walls were pushed out to increase the size of the blossoming metropolis. Church construction also experienced a boom during this period, with local masons enjoying a period of high employment unheard of during any age since that time. Gothic architecture was the style of choice, with examples evident in the designs of the Duomo, Santa Maria Donnaregina, San Lorenzo and Sant'Eligio.

Baroque splendour in Via Toledo

THE PALAZZI OF VIA TOLEDO

A walk down the Via Toledo today will confront you with a plethora of high-street shops, department stores, cafés and *tabacchi* alcoves. Yet it wasn't always like this. Via Toledo used to be the address of choice for the rich and powerful of the city.

The popularity of Via Toledo as a place to live occurred following the extension of the city walls during the Renaissance. Today, most of the grand structures are crumbling and far from their prime, but you can still glimpse signs of former grandeur in the form of the Rinascente Department Store at No 340 (once known as the Palazzo Buono), the Palazzo Berio (No 256) and the Palazzo Barbaja (No 205), which was once home to composer Gioacchino Rossini of *The Barber of Seville* opera fame.

The Renaissance left its mark on the city in many ways during the period of the Aragon court: the finest documentation of the movement is in the *Tavola Strozzi*, located in the Certosa di San Martino museum.

Baroque bonanza

Never before or since has an architectural or design aesthetic captured the Neapolitan attitude as much as the Baroque period. The fantastical and ostentatious elements of Baroque combined perfectly with the Neapolitan flair for the dramatic. As such, the city is awash with examples of Baroque fancy. From the stunning Reggia at Caserta, built by Vanvitelli for the royal family of Naples, to the

Santa Maria del Purgatorio

grotesque skulls littering the front of the church of Santa Maria del Purgatorio, Naples can sometimes resemble a celebration of the extreme – all characteristic of this decidedly ostentatious and sometimes gaudy period in architectural history.

Piazza Dante, the San Carlo opera house, Albergo dei Poveri (Europe's largest ever civic construction) and the imposing Palazzo Reale all date their births to the years of the Bourbon dynasty when passions and coffers overflowed.

Architectural big names to look out for include Vaccaro, the aforementioned Vanvitelli, Fuga, Sanfelice and Medrano. Most of the major Baroque projects of the time can be attributed to one of these big names in building design.

HUNTING FOR GLAMOUR

Naples owes much of its stunning Baroque architecture to the Bourbon family's love of a good hunt. Determined to bag as many trophies as they possibly could, architects were hired by the noble classes to build the Reggia at Caserta and the stunning villas along the Miglio d'Oro in order to provide easy access to the countryside. Today, the Reggia rivals Versailles in terms of both size and scope. The Italian armed forces now claim many of the rooms in the palace for administrative purposes, so I guess you could say that guns remain an important fixture in this regal residence of times past.

Palatial paradise: Reggia

Onwards from Napoleon

Following Napoleon's successful capture of the city in the early 19th century, Naples went into an architectural decline that has remained until the present day. French forces, in an effort to control the disease and crowded conditions of the city, focused most of their energies on urban renewal, wiping out hundreds of dilapidated neighbourhoods in order to replace them with open areas, squares and gardens in a neoclassical style. The seafront found a new lease of life, with the Chiaia district announcing its status as a favourable address – an honour it has yet to give up. And engineering feats like the invention of the funicular opened up high-ground locations like Vomero to residential development.

Following the destructive bombs of World War II, developers either rebuilt ancient structures according to original plans or replaced entire neighbourhoods with horrific modern eyesores much denounced by locals. Residents had little say in what was going up around them during this boom period, as most of the construction blueprints were in the hands of the mafia and the pockets of local government. Huge council-housing estates in the suburbs of the city transformed the outskirts into crime-filled wastelands of poverty, while factories gutted the seashore – convenient for the dumping of pollution and waste, but not so attractive for the average tourist to look at.

Notable buildings from this period include the horrific Jolly Hotel complex, the abandoned steelworks at Bagnoli and the massive Centro Direzionale project of the 1980s.

Albergo di Poveri

Neapolitans have always loved their theatre – perhaps because their everyday life often resembles a life-size stage. Dramatic origins date back to the time of Nero when the fanciful emperor would take himself off to catch some of the ribald Roman comedies of the day. The popular Neapolitan theatrical form of commedia dell'arte can trace its origins back to this early form of entertainment in that both the early Roman theatre and *commedia* are based around stock characters and the use of masks which indicate differences in identity and emotion.

Commedia dell'arte found its feet in the 16th century when Renaissance tastes demanded a new outlet for their entertainment pleasure. Neapolitan mask and acting traditions were revived by the local acting trade, resulting in wild, eye-boggling concoctions of scripted and improvised delight. Characters in *commedia* were given the characteristics associated with different

Italian cities, with Naples providing the much-loved figures of Pulcinella (the foul-mouthed, white-clad clown and symbol of the city) and Scaramouche (a Spanish captain known for his constant bragging and cowardice). Pulcinella figurines are one of the most popular souvenirs brought home by visitors to the city. You'll spot the tiny statues depicting the lovable and carefree scamp at almost every purveyor of tourist tat. Just look for the whimsical figure dressed in a white smock and trousers with a white dunce's cap for a hat and red-and-yellow-striped shoes.

If you're very lucky, there may even

be a performance of commedia at Naples' most famous venue for the performing arts, the Teatro di San Carlo (although its dedication towards dance and opera makes this an extremely rare occurrence). Originally built in 1731 and rebuilt following a fire in 1816, San Carlo is

TEATRO DI SAN CARLO
1737
STAGIONE D'OPERA E DI BALLETTO 2000

I DUE FOSCARI
di Giuseppe Verdi

Novembre: 8 - 10 - 12 - 14 - 16 - 19

Italy's oldest theatre and second in prominence only to Milan's La Scala. Shoestring budgets always loom over the producers of the theatre, with foreclosure a seemingly ever-present threat to the Teatro di San Carlo's ongoing survival, yet somehow the show always manages to go on – and the results are invariably stunning.

Openings at the San Carlo bring out the city's glitterati and are always the highpoint of the city's social calendar. While programming remains somewhat traditional, in the last couple of seasons attempts have been made to invigorate staging through the use of prominent visual artists such as David Hockney, or up-and-coming young directors.

The opera season runs throughout the year, with a two-month stoppage during the summer months because of the hot weather – there is no air conditioning anywhere inside the venue. A subscription ticketing system means that seats for all performances are difficult to come by. If you go to the box office on the off chance of buying a couple of tickets, you will most likely be presented with the option of purchasing the worst seats in the house – the staff aren't being vindictive, they just don't have anything else they can sell you.

As for attire, think smart-casual. You won't find black-tie in the audience (with the exception of opening night); however, jeans and T-shirts will draw evil glares from the well-heeled crowds around you. Guided tours of the building are available, in the event that you can't score an elusive pair of tickets.

Teatro di San Carlo, Via San Carlo 98F. Tel: (081) 797 2412. www.teatrosancarlo.it. Open: Box Office Sept–June Tue–Sun 10am–3pm; July Tue–Fri 10am–3pm; 1hr before curtain up. Performance times and dates vary. Charge for tickets and tours. Bus 24, C22, C25, C57.

This page and opposite: the interior and exterior of the Teatro di San Carlo

Roman and Ancient Sites

If archaeologists could have their way, the entire top metre of buildings, soil, dirt and residences that cover the city of Naples would be removed to give access to what lies beneath. A treasure trove of Greek and Roman remains lies under the city, almost, but not quite, within reach of scholars of the classical age.

Roman frescoes

Very little has been excavated, mainly due to the fact that it is almost impossible to dig up anywhere under the crowded and delicate streets that comprise the bulk of the Centro Storico. One wrong hole and an entire street could plummet into the ground below. One group that does its best to open up the mysteries of the earth is the Napoli Sotteranea. With their support a number of churches, including the Santa Chiara, Duomo, Santa Maria in Purgatorio ad Arco and San Lorenzo, have opened up sections of their grounds to give a peek at what lies below.

For the best ancient sites, you'll have to get yourself out of town. In addition to the world-renowned excavations at Pompeii and Herculaneum, there is evidence of Roman splendour dotted throughout the countryside – a testament to a time when the Campanian coast was a playground for the rich and famous of the day. The town of Baia and the Phlegraean Fields were particularly well loved by the upper classes for their famed curative waters. The geothermally heated spas and baths were favoured by a number of leaders, including Hadrian, Claudius, Nero and Caligula. Citizens looking for higher social standing and favours from the throne flocked to the area during the summer months, when the warm weather and cooling breezes attracted a who's who of Roman government. As such, the area established a reputation for gluttony, excess and ostentatious displays of wealth. It also became a favourite getaway for adulterous couples, and a place for sexual experimentation.

Emperor Tiberius loved the area so much that he temporarily moved his home to Capri, setting up house in the Villa Jovis on the eastern tip of the island. While little remains that suggests the level of splendour that once covered the Villa, a little bit of imagination should be enough to paint the frescoes and gilt work that once covered the region.

For a brief glimpse of the original 4th-century BC Greek city walls, hop over to the centre of Piazza Bellini. There isn't much to see, but the ruins give you an idea of just how far the city of Naples has spread since its days as the picturesque seaside port of Neapolis.

SIBYLLINE SUPERSTITION

Campania has always produced its fair share of savvy wheelers and dealers, but never more so than the God Apollo's best-ever spokeswoman, the Sibyl of Cuma. Legend has it that in the 5th century BC, the Cuman Sibyl attempted to get her God more noticed by the Roman authorities. In a canny bit of Neapolitan mercantilism, the Sibyl asked for an outrageous amount of money when she travelled to Rome to sell her nine books of Apollo's prophecies to the Roman King Tarquinius. Each time she was refused, the Sibyl calmly threw three of the books into a fire. When she was left with three books, the superstitious King relented and the Cuman Sibyl got her original asking price. From that moment on, Apollo became an important God in the pantheon of Roman deities.

Acropoli di Cuma, Via Montecuma, Cuma. Tel: (081) 854 3060. Open: daily 9am–1hr before sunset. Admission charge.

Bellissima Piazza Bellini

Paris has the Louvre. Madrid boasts the Prado. And London has the British Museum. For Naples, the crown jewel of museums must be the Museo Nazionale Archeologico. Home to one of the world's largest collections of Roman and ancient artefacts, the Museo holds many treasures excavated from the digs of Herculaneum, Pompeii and Stabiae, as well as numerous other must-sees drawn from the sea-based empires of the Mediterranean that once ruled the world.

Formerly home to Naples University, King Ferdinand I transformed this massive four-storey *palazzo* into a museum after inheriting a number of ancient pieces from his grandmother. Following the discovery of Pompeii, the rooms filled up fast. Today's museum only exhibits a fraction of what is actually owned. Collections include a vast selection of Egyptian objects, many of which were transported to Italy and unearthed in digs in the Campania region, an excess of Greek busts and statuary, intricate mosaics and a scandalous room of ancient pornography.

Reopened in 2000, the decidedly soft-core *Gabinetto segreto* (Secret cabinet) boasts a number of blush-inducing images, including a range of phallic talismans, a collection of erect Pan sculptures and explicit paintings and mosaics removed from the private bedrooms of some of Pompeii's richest citizens. Note that this collection is off limits to anyone under the age of 11 and is watched by a small gaggle of female attendants at all times.

The bulk of the treasures plundered from Herculaneum and Pompeii can be

found on the first floor of the museum, centred on the Sala Meridiana. This may change at any moment, however, as constant upkeep and renovation keep the rooms moving around, depending upon construction schedules. From the Sala, the first few rooms you pass through hold silverware, pottery, glassware

and other decorative and everyday household objects. In Rooms 114 to 117, just before the entrance to the Sala, all the artefacts are from the Villa dei Papiri in Herculaneum. Vases, bowls and urns can be found in the second set of rooms on the right. All of these objects are from sites further afield in southern Italy.

A large collection of Palaeolithic, Neolithic and Bronze Age items, dating back to 100,000 BC, is located along the third corridor on the right from the Sala Meridiana. Stone flints and funerary offerings are arranged in location order, with the best finds coming from the necropolis of Capri. If busts and statues are your passion, stick to the ground floor's Farnese collection. The powerful Farnese family pilfered a ton of treasures from ancient sites in Rome during the 16th century. Pope Paul III, otherwise known as Alessandro Farnese, filtered many of the Church's ancient holdings into the hands of his influential clan.

While the Farnese paintings are holed up in the Capodimonte museum just up

the street, the heavier marble items featuring characters from Greek and Roman legend and society can be found in the rooms just off the main open-air heart of the museum, directly in front of the main entrance.

Modern and visiting exhibits are another factor in museum geography, with big-name shows usually housed in the vast rooms on the ground floor, to the right of the ticket office.

Piazza Museo Archeologico, Piazza Museo 19. Tel: (081) 564 8941. www.archeona.arti.beniculturali.it. Open: Museum Mon, Wed–Sun 9am–7.30pm; ticket office closes 1hr earlier. Gabinetto segreto Mon, Wed–Sun 9.30am–1.30pm, 2.30–6.30pm. Guided tours every 30min. Admission charge. Metro Cavour or Museo. Bus 47, CS, E1.

This page and above left: Mosaic, fresco and stone relief from the collection
Below left: Museo Nazionale Archeologico

Palazzi and Castles

A centre for nobility and royalty almost since the day the city was founded, Naples has a wide variety of castles, palazzi and regal residences. While many of the homes of the ancient rich and famous have been transformed into shops and museums, you can still catch a glimpse of what regal living was once like in a number of well-restored locations throughout the city.

Old Napoli

Architectural styles used in the construction of these heavenly homes depend strictly on the fashions of the period when they were designed, so you can expect everything from a crumbling Norman edifice to a wedding-cake structure of Baroque splendour in your explorations.

Castel dell'Ovo

Naples' oldest castle, this imposing seafront castle boasts over a thousand years of history. Built during the Norman period, Castel dell'Ovo was originally intended for military use, defending the city from the almost constant threat of invasion and terror. Its site was always an important location in Neapolitan history – it originally held a monastic community during the Middle Ages. Before that, it was a treasured section of the grounds owned by the Roman general Lucullus. Legend says that Castel dell'Ovo derived its name from the Roman period when the poet Virgil stayed as a guest of Lucullus. According to tradition, Virgil buried an egg in the ground, predicting doom and gloom should the egg ever break.

Many of the rooms in the Castel dell'Ovo are in use as offices; however, there are still large sections of the structure undergoing restoration. Even when there are crowds of tourists, the castle can feel strangely deserted. To get the most out of it, lose yourself in the maze of quiet passageways and landings, making sure you climb up the long ramp inside the castle to enjoy the views of the Bay below.
Via Partenope. Tel: (081) 246 4111. Open: Mon–Sat 9am–6pm; Sun 9am–1.30pm. Bus 140, C24, C25, C28, R3. Tram 1.

Castel Nuovo

Built in 1279 by Charles of Anjou, the Castel Nuovo (New Castle) was the Angevin residence and fortress of choice. Little of the original decoration exists inside the castle walls, thanks to a series of alterations performed during the age of the Aragonese (15th century).

During its Angevin heyday, the Castel Nuovo was a centre for the arts, with beacons of the worlds of literature and visual art drawn to the Neapolitan court. Boccaccio's epic collection of

Italian lore, *The Decameron*, was written during this period, as well as a number of short stories set in and around the city of Naples. In addition, Giotto famously frescoed the castle's chapel and main entrance hall. Unfortunately, little of Giotto's work remains on display, with the exception of the work found on the ceiling of the *Sala dei Baroni* (Room of the Barons) – scene of Naples' rambunctious city council meetings. While the council meetings have a tendency to get vicious, they will never be as deadly as the events in 1486 when a group of mutinous barons was murdered by King Ferrante, thus giving the room its name.

For authentic Angevin architecture, your best option is the **Cappella Palatina** – it is the only section of this castle that was left untouched by the meddling Aragonese.

Preparations are underway to continue with restorations of the castle, including plans to open up the dungeons, construct a lift in the northeastern tower and excavate the **Fossa del Crocodrillo** (Drain of the Crocodiles) – a room in which a large crocodile apparently devoured particularly dangerous enemies of the state.

Piazza Municipio. Tel: (081) 795 2003. Open: June–Mar Mon–Sat 9am–7pm. Apr, May Mon–Sat 9am–7pm; Sun 9am–2pm; ticket office closes 1hr earlier. Admission charge. Bus C25, E3, R1, R2, R3. Tram 1.

Inside the Palazzo dello Spagnolo

Castel Sant'Elmo

The Castel Sant'Elmo boasts what are probably Naples' most glorious views. While not the original structure, the current building owes much of its look to additions made in the 16th century when it gained its six-pointed star shape. A castle has existed at this strategic location overlooking the Bay of Naples since 1329, when King Robert of Anjou constructed a fortification above a small church dedicated to St Erasmus, or 'Elmo' – hence the name.

A walk through the castle can be strangely spooky, especially during the gloomy winter months. A spacious modern and experimental art collection takes up many of the interior spaces, including the dungeons on the first floor – some of which were still being used for military prisoners until as recently as the 1970s. The top floor, otherwise known as the **Piazza d'Armi**, acts as the roof of the castle, from which you can obtain breathtaking views of the city below.

Via Tito Angelini 22. Tel: (081) 578 4030. Open: Tue–Sun 9am–7.30pm; ticket office closes 1hr earlier. Admission charge. Funicular Montesanto to Via Morghen, Centrale to Piazzetta Fuga or Chiaia to Via Cimarosa. Bus V1.

Palazzo Reale

This is Naples' most famous royal residence. Construction on the building began in 1600, taking two years to complete (although some finishing touches were still being added 50 years later). Designed by Neapolitan architect Domenico Fontana, the Royal Palace was constructed for the Spanish viceroys who dominated the city during much of the 17th century. One of the only residences in the city where original frescoes, paintings, furnishings and fixtures are still in their rightful place, the current interiors possess a neoclassical appearance, thanks largely to the French tastes of the 19th century, when entire wings were gutted at the pleasure of the Napoleonic rulers.

While the art collections are largely unimpressive, the **Teatrino di Corte** (a small, private theatre) and **Biblioteca Nazionale** are worth keeping an eye out for. The biblioteca's collection of manuscripts and books is impressive, with some works dating back to the 5th century.

Access to the ticket office is badly marked. Look for the room to the left

Palazzo Reale

of the main entrance in order to get into the apartments located at the top of the staircase.

Piazza del Plebiscito. Tel: (081) 794 4021. Open: Mon, Tue, Thur–Sun 9am–8pm; ticket office closes 1hr earlier. Admission charge. Bus 24, C22, C82, R2, R3.

Palazzo Serra di Cassano

This beautifully restored palazzo features a brilliant grey double stairway built out of the volcanic rock indigenous to the area. An individual appointment is the only way you can take a peek into the frescoed apartments, many of which feature original furniture. Today, the palazzo houses the Italian Institute for Philosophical Studies.

Via Monte di Dio 14. Tel: (081) 245 2150. www.iisf.it. Open: by appointment. Bus C22.

From the Fascist era: Palazzo delle Poste

Churches

If you think that there's a church on every corner in Naples, then you'd probably be right. While many churches are still used as houses of worship, over 50 per cent of Neapolitan religious centres are boarded up – whether due to flood, bombings, fatigue or earthquake.

Duomo door

When visiting a church, it is best to be soberly attired – remember these sites are active places of religious practice. Try not to visit during mass unless you feel you can blend in with the congregation. Masses are always conducted in Italian or Latin, so if you don't speak the lingo then you may be at a loss trying to follow the service.

Duomo

The main cathedral of Naples, the Duomo, can trace its history back to the 4th century. The current structure was built over what was once the church of Santa Stefania in the latter half of the 13th century. While the exterior fails to impress, the internal magnificence will be sure to take your breath away. Gilt covers almost every inch of the vaulted ceiling, while paintings by noted artist Luca Giordano, located between the various windows and arches, tell biblical stories and illuminate the figure of Christ.

The real draw is in the large chapel on the right. The **Cappella di San Gennaro** contains numerous artefacts, statues and busts dedicated to the patron saint of Naples, San Gennaro. Most of the really stunning items are only put on display during May and September in preparation for the big days when San Gennaro's blood transforms into a liquid from its congealed state. During these sacred calendar dates, the Duomo holds a sea of worshippers, praying feverishly to bring luck (and liquid) to the auspicious occasion.

San Gennaro's skull bones and two phials of blood are kept in a 14th-century silver bust, which is locked permanently in a strongbox behind the altar.

Via Duomo 147. Tel: (081) 449 097. www.duomodinapoli.com. Open: Church Mon–Sat 8am–12.30pm, 4.30–7pm; Sun 8am–1.30pm, 5–7.30pm. Collections and baptistery Mon–Sat 9am–noon, 4.30–6.30pm; Sun 8.30am–1pm. Admission charge for collections and baptistery. Bus E1, R2.

Gesù Nuovo

Originally a palazzo, this church is notable for its façade of raised, diamond-shaped stone. The interiors were transformed from a place of residence to a place of worship in the 16th century by architect Giuseppe Valeriani. Of particular interest is a room dedicated to local saint Giuseppe Moscati, a 20th-century Neapolitan doctor who forsook the trappings of wealth and prestige in order to tend to the health of the local poor.

Piazza del Gesù 2. Tel: (081) 551 8613. Open: Mon–Sat 7am–12.30pm, 4–7pm; Sun 7am–2pm, 4–7pm. Metro Montesanto or Dante. Bus E1, R1.

San Lorenzo Maggiore

This extremely popular church was restored back to its original 13th-century form following extensive postwar renovation. While the façade makes the church look decidedly Baroque in construction, this is merely a superficial addition to the original Gothic design – a change made to reflect the tastes of the

period and the Neapolitan love affair with anything ostentatious. Readers of Naples' answer to *The Canterbury Tales*, the *Decameron*, should note that it was within these church walls that Boccaccio fell in love with Fiammetta. Be sure not to miss the original mosaic flooring preserved under glass in the transept.

Via dei Tribunali 316. Tel: (081) 454 948. Open: daily 8am–noon, 5–7pm. Metro Montesanto or Dante. Bus E1.

Sant'Anna dei Lombardi

The most notable Renaissance church in a city not known for its Renaissance architecture, this church is worth

Exploring the San Gregario Armeno

Tower of San Domenico Maggiore

including on your itinerary, in order to examine the unique inlaid wooden panels that line the walls and the collection of terracotta statues by Guido Mazzoni entitled *Mourning the Death of Christ*.
Piazza Monteoliveto 14.
Tel: (081) 551 3333. Open: Tue–Sat 9am–12.30pm. Metro Montesanto. Bus E1, R1, R4.

Santa Chiara

This Gothic church was built during the reign of Robert of Anjou. Bomb attacks and Baroque reconstruction have done much to reduce this place of worship favoured by the aristocracy – following World War II, all that was left were the four church walls.

Go past the cloister for a look at salvaged pieces from the original 14th-century structure, shards of

bomb shrapnel and excavations below the surface that reveal a gymnasium and baths from the age of the Roman Empire.
Via Benedetto Croce. Tel: Church (081) 552 6280, Museum (081) 552 1597. Open: Church daily 8am–12.30pm, 4.30–7.30pm. Museum and cloister Mon–Sat 9.30am–1pm, 2.30–5.30pm; Sun 9.30am–1pm. Admission charge to enter museum and cloister. Metro Montesanto or Dante. Bus E1.

Santa Maria del Purgatorio ad Arco

A decidedly eerie church – and one that has captured the imaginations of the thoroughly superstitious Neapolitan population – Santa Maria del Purgatorio ad Arco is also known as the 'death's head' church, on account of the three bronze skulls that sit outside its railings. During periods of famine, plague and war, Neapolitan women adopted skulls and cared for them in place of loved and lost menfolk. Today, adopted skulls are used to request divine favours and intercession. While this tradition is banned as idolatrous by the Catholic Church, the practice is said to live on.
Via dei Tribunali 39. Tel: (081) 292 622. Open: Mon–Sat 9am–1pm. Metro Montesanto or Dante. Bus E1.

Santa Maria Donnaregina

The condition of Santa Maria Donnaregina owes much to the fact that it was decidedly out of favour and abandoned for 250 years from the 1600s to the 1850s. Due to the public preference for the 17th-century church located right next door, Santa Maria's frescoes, interiors and Gothic

architecture were left untouched – the result is one of Naples' most authentic churches.
Vico Donnaregina 26.
Tel/Fax: (081) 299 101. Open: by appointment. Bus E1.

Interior of the Duomo

Santissima Annunziata

The Annunziata complex of fountains, courtyards and an adjoining orphanage dates back to the 14th century; however, the church owes its manifestation to the designs of Vanvitelli (famous for his Reggia in Caserta). Details to note are the fine majolica clock that dominates the bell tower over the entrance, the 16th-century wooden doors, and a foundling wheel that was still in use until the 1980s. Unwanted children would be placed in the foundling wheel for acceptance by the orphanage directors, with abandoned children given the name *Esposito* (meaning 'laid before God's mercy'). You may notice locals avoid the foundling wheel at all costs. Many still associate its presence with hard times when unwanted and unaffordable pregnancies resulted in starvation and stigma.
Via dell'Annunziata 34.
Tel: (081) 207 455.
Open: Wheel Mon–Sat 9am–1pm; Church closed for restoration. Metro: Garibaldi. Bus R2. Tram 1.

Museums and Galleries

Other than the phenomenal Museo Nazionale Archeologico, Naples isn't really a museum town. Residents prefer to enjoy their artefacts on the sun-drenched streets – and when you have over 3,000 years of history surrounding you, who needs a cooped-up, dust-covered gallery to enjoy it in. Despite this fact, there are still a number of collections worth looking at – perfect for those rare days when rain hits the city.

Capodimonte

Certosa-Museo di San Martino
The Museo di San Martino boasts one of the most intriguing collections of treasures in the city. To its credit, San Martino is more than just a museum. A former monastery, the grounds of the Certosa-Museo hold an art gallery, a collection of Nativity scenes and a spectacular church, in addition to the aforementioned museum. The highlight of the collection is the fascinating *Tavola Strozzi* – a 3-D depiction of the city of Naples as it looked in the 15th century. Familiar buildings, including the Castel Nuovo and the Certosa, can be seen if you look hard enough.
Largo San Martino 5.
Tel/Fax: (081) 578 1769. Open: Tue–Sat 8.30am–7.30pm, Sun 9am–7.30pm. Admission charge. Funicular Montesanto to Via Morghen, Centrale to Piazzetta Fuga or Chiaia to Via Cimarosa. Bus V1.

Musei Inter-dipartimenti
A collection of four natural history museums owned and operated by Naples University. Subjects covered include geology, mineralogy, palaeontology, anthropology and zoology. The zoology museum is a particular favourite with children.
Via Mezzocannone 8. Tel: (081) 253 7516. www.musei.unina.it. Open: Mon 9am–1.30pm, 3–5pm; Tue–Fri 9am–1.30pm; Sat, Sun 9am–1pm. Admission charge. Bus 14, CD, E1, R2.

Museo Civico Filangieri
The Museo Civico Filangieri chronicles the history of industrial design, with over 3,000 items of household interest, clothing and costume, weaponry, coins and chinaware lovingly displayed for fans of the applied and fine arts. Paintings and sculpture are also included in the collection – pieced together by Prince Gaetano Filangieri in 1882 – most of which date from between the 14th and 19th centuries.
Via Duomo 288A. Tel: (081) 203 211. Closed indefinitely for restoration. Call ahead for details.

Museo di Capodimonte
Naples' 'other' great art collection, the Museo di Capodimonte, is the

A more modern 'fresco'

sister museum to the Museo Nazionale in that it holds the great paintings of the celebrated Farnese collection. Many would argue that Capodimonte got the better pieces to showcase, including a number by Raphael and Titian. The climax of the first floor is Titian's *Danae*, located in Room 11. Painted for the sleeping chambers of a Cardinal, this ambitious masterpiece is surprisingly erotic, portraying the naked Danae seduced by Jupiter. Other big names featured at the Capodimonte include Botticelli, El Greco, Renoir, Caravaggio, Rembrandt, Tintoretto and a couple of fine Brueghels.
Via Capodimonte.
Tel: (081) 749 9111. Open: Tue–Sat 10am–7pm, Sun 9am–2pm. Admission charge. Bus 24, 110, R4.

Museo Nazionale della Ceramica Duca di Martina

The world of ceramics is celebrated in this museum. The first floor is dedicated to the history of European work, including work from Meissen and obligatory examples of fine Capodimonte figurines. The ground level holds international work, with a focus on Japanese and Chinese pieces.
Via Cimarosa 77.
Tel: (081) 578 1776. Open: Guided tours only, Tue–Sun 9.30am, 11am, 12.30pm. Admission charge. Funicular Montesanto to Via Morghen, Centrale to Piazzetta Fuga or Chiaia to Via Cimarosa. Bus E4, V1.

While the Catholic Church would like you to think otherwise, superstition and luck have a powerful hold over the minds of the average Neapolitan. On many street corners you will find tarot readers plying their trade, and many residents pay a visit to their favourite fortune-tellers as often as they go out to get a loaf of bread.

Misfortune and destruction – specifically in the form of earthquakes and volcanoes – while scientifically proven to be caused by the geological faults and volcanic activity in the area, are often blamed on the supernatural. Keeping your *monacello* (house spirit) happy is one way to ensure your continued good fortune. Taking the form of a mischievous little boy, the *monacello* tells your fortune depending on what he chooses to wear. If he is dressed in white, then you have a bountiful future. Red, however, means impending doom.

The 'evil eye' is still thought of as an everyday problem. One common method by which those afflicted with bad mojo remove the problem is through a local TV show on which local *maghi* (magicians) appear so that people can ring in and ask for their evil spirits to be removed. If a *maghi* isn't available and a Neapolitan feels like they've had an encounter with a *jettatore* (spell caster), then their best course of action is to touch iron, or a horn of gold, coral or silver. 'Making horns' by pointing the index and forefinger at a suspected caster is another sure-fire preventative measure, although it is also highly offensive if performed on an innocent bystander.

Small pieces of horn or iron in the shape of a smiling *jettatore* are available from most souvenir stores if you feel the need for a bit of luck. Taxi drivers are particularly well stocked with charms,

mainly due to the poor driving habits of the city's inhabitants. Historically, extreme poverty and natural disasters have provided Neapolitans with good reasons to believe in anything they can in order to survive. This explains why the lottery proved to be extremely popular when it was first introduced. After all, what other organisation combined the superstitious power of numbers with the opportunity to get rich? Neapolitans play the lottery with a fervour seen only in the most dedicated of religious followers. There are 90 numbers to choose from, with many locals refusing to leave the country whenever a big draw is approaching or tell even their closest relations their favourite series of digits. As expected in superstitious Naples, all of the numbers in *Il Lotto* hold a specific meaning in order to assist with their selection. A handbook known as the *smorfia*, which outlines the separate meanings, details the language of the numbers in relation to nightly dreams. If you need help picking the right combination, go along to any lotto office and relay the details of your dreams to the ticket seller, who will then analyse the dreams and find the right numbers that match the images. Some of the more intriguing numbers include 85 (Souls of Purgatory), 45 (wine), 76 (fountain) and 2 (little girl). There are even selections available should your dreams prove to be X-rated, including 28 (breasts), 29 (penis) and 16 (bum).

Opposite: A view down Spaccanopoli
Below: The Guglia dell'Immacolata

Centro Storico

The historic heart of the city, the Centro Storico is the district of Naples most visitors think of first. It is here where you will find the bulk of the city's oldest treasures, including the Duomo and the ancient Greek neighbourhood of Spaccanapoli. Geographically, the Centro Storico is tiny, yet its population density is amongst the highest in Europe.

Gesù Nuovo

Tiny streets and alleyways weave through the district, with precariously constructed buildings packed into every possible inch of space. A number of times throughout its history, the Centro Storico has come under threat from urban regeneration planners and health and safety operatives – it has also been host to a number of plagues throughout its precarious past. Today, the neighbourhood remains the rubbish-choked, overcrowded mess has always been. Keep one eye on the beautiful sight around you and one eye plastered on the ground to see where you're stepping, in order fully to appreciate this fascinating quarter.

City walls

Until the mid-17th century, the city of Naples was firmly contained within its city walls. Unchanged for almost 2,000 years, the walls were considered essential by the Norman king Roger in 1140, yet proved to be a serious problem to future generations as the minute space within the walls stifled development and caused serious overcrowding. Little remains of the walls today, the best remaining stretch occurring at the **Porta Capuana** gate – a triumphal arch and series of towers dating back to 1484 and situated at the eastern end of Spaccanapoli.

Spaccanapoli

The original Greek and Roman heart of the city, this is where the city of Neapolis took form to become the metropolis of today. Spaccanapoli is not so much an area as it is a name for the ancient *decumanus inferior* – a series of streets that made up the centre of Naples. If today's planners were as smart as the first Greeks, then the city would be planned on a grid system just like it was in times of old. The bulk of Spaccanapoli is now pedestrianised, although you will often find a number of cheeky scooter-drivers making a break for it when the city becomes too clogged to move through. The shops that line the streets follow ancient patterns: around the university you will find a number of bookshops, stationery shops and purveyors of musical instruments – many of which have existed in the same location for generations. Religious artefact shops, pricey jewellers and souvenir stores are usually located near churches and other tourist hot spots.

Via San Gregorio Armeno

Housing a fine collection of souvenir shops, this delicate street runs downhill from the Via Dei Tribunali towards the State Archives. The savvy shopkeepers of San Gregorio know that their salaries are in the hands of the tourists, so lunch-hour closures are uncommon. Everything from *Pulcinella* figurines to light-up Nativity crèches is available for sale, albeit at a vastly inflated price. An abundance of striped awnings makes shopping a possibility on even the most rain-choked of days. Good for browsing and the occasional impulse purchase.

The columns of San Paolo Maggiore

Walk: The Bloody Miracles of Centro Storico

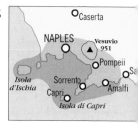

On this walk, we discover the world of Naples' patron saint, San Gennaro. As befits a man of holy inklings, most of the sites are religious in aspect – including a number of working churches. If you plan on entering active places of worship, be sure to wear appropriate attire.

The walk starts at the Duomo located on Via Duomo, just north of the Via Dei Tribunali.

Allow 2 hours.

1 Duomo

(*See p42 for details*) Walk into the Duomo and explore the large chapel on the right. It contains a number of artefacts dedicated to San Gennaro, including the famous blood that liquefies three times a year.
Via Duomo 147. Tel: (081) 449 097. www.duomodinapoli.com. Open: Church Mon–Sat 8am–12.30pm, 4.30–7pm; Sun 8am–1.30pm, 5–7.30pm. Collections and baptistery Mon–Sat 9am–noon,

Patron saint San Gennaro

4.30–6.30pm; Sun 8.30am–1pm. Admission charge for collections and baptistery.
Turn left out of the Duomo main doors and take a right at Via Dei Tribunali.

2 San Lorenzo Maggiore

Home to the blood of San Lorenzo – perpetually found in a liquid state.
Via dei Tribunali 316. Tel: (081) 454 948. Open: daily 8am–noon, 5–7pm.
Continue along Via Dei Tribunali.
Turn left onto Via San Gregorio Armeno.

3 San Gregorio Armeno

Santa Patrizia, San Giovanni Battista and San Panteleone's liquefying blood are kept in this important basilica. Santa Patrizia was the niece of a Byzantine emperor who died a virgin after fleeing from unwanted male attention in her homeland. Her blood liquefies every Tuesday morning and on 25 August.
Via San Gregorio Armeno 1.
Tel: (081) 552 0186. Open: Mon, Wed–Fri 9am–noon; Tue 9am–12.45pm; Sat, Sun 9am–12.30pm.
Continue down San Gregorio Armeno.

Inside the San Gregorio Armeno

4 Via San Gregorio Armeno

(See p51 for details) Turn right at the end of the street onto Via San Biagio. Continue along walking past Piazzetta Nilo until you reach Via Benedetto Croce.

5 Via Benedetto Croce

A street of jewellers chock-full of beautifully worked Italian gold and precious stone dealers.

Slowly browse along the Via San Benedetto Croce. Santa Chiara will be on the left just before you reach the Piazza Gesù Nuovo.

6 Santa Chiara

(See p44 for details) Via Benedetto Croce. Tel: Church (081) 552 6280, Museum (081) 552 1597. Open: Church daily 8am–12.30pm, 4.30–7.30pm. Museum and cloister Mon–Sat 9.30am–1pm, 2.30–5.30pm; Sun 9.30am–1pm. Admission charge to enter museum and cloister.

Cross the street from the main entrance to reach Gesù Nuovo.

7 Gesù Nuovo

(See p42 for details) Piazza del Gesù 2. Tel: (081) 551 8613. Open: Mon–Sat 7am–12.30pm, 4–7pm; Sun 7am–2pm, 4–7pm.
Backtrack along Via Benedetto Croce and take the first left, which is Via San Sebastiano. Continue until you reach Piazza Bellini.

8 Coffee in Piazza Bellini

A favourite Neapolitan watering hole, this welcoming collection of cafés and bookstores is a popular late-night drinking and people-watching spot that keeps going well into the evening. Toast your pedestrian success with a well-earned coffee at any of the cafés that line this leafy square.

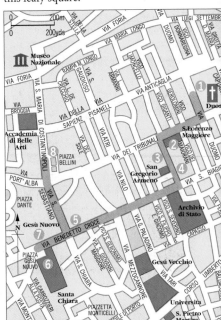

The history of organised crime in Naples dates back centuries; however, the large-scale criminal activity associated with the crime-lords of today is a far cry from the relatively gentle smuggling and theft that made up the bulk of profits until the closing days of World War II. Known by the ancient Spanish name of *La Camorra*, local mafia hoods were primarily involved in two-bit operations until the arrival of crime-boss Raffaele Cutolo during the mid-1970s. Up until then, organised crime units occupied themselves with profits made from cigarette, fruit and vegetable smuggling. Cutolo upped the ante by creating his *Nuova Camorra Organizzata*. Clans that failed to join his band of merry men were forced to join together under the banner of the *Nuova Famiglia Unita*. The two organisations have been battling between themselves for control of the city ever since. Cutolo is famous for soaking up millions of lire in reconstruction money following the earthquake of 1980, leaving thousands homeless and numerous housing projects unfinished as funds ran dry. Police did much to attack the *camorra* clans after evidence of their post-earthquake racketeering came to light, only to find that the groups fractured into a number of smaller-scale families willing to fight to the death for their pockets of neighbourhood control.

The darkest years occurred between 1983 and 1993, when ten mayors in a row failed to do anything to crack the hold the *camorra* had on everything from basic public services to the street tobacco trade. Strikes dictated by the *camorra* leadership were a common problem, specifically involving employees of the city's rubbish collection companies. Rubbish and well-fed rats lined the crowded streets during these disease-ridden periods of action, crippling the police forces and any honest government leaders who might happen to care about the state of the city.

Property development and construction are the two industries in which the bulk of illegal profits have been made. Numerous poorly-designed projects and buildings sprouted up throughout the chaotic postwar period, much to the chagrin (and secret financial delight) of city councillors. Despite the introduction of hundreds of building codes and laws designed to prevent an explosion in mismanaged architecture, local leaders often turned a blind eye as their wallets were lined with kickback money which was provided with the compliments of their friendly, neighbourhood criminal clans.

The year 1992 proved to be the end of the line for the gravy train, as the *Mani pulite* (clean hands) campaign swept a number of corrupt practices and politicians out of office and into the criminal courts. However, now that local government is proving not to be above a bit of backhanding, the *camorra* is evolving yet again. Recent scams that keep the police busy include illegal prescription drug distribution, the sale of faulty second-hand airline parts and a complex con involving cloned southern Italian number plates, registration papers and insurance details sold to northern Italian drivers, thus enabling them to collect endless traffic and parking fines – only for the final bill to be sent to the unsuspecting southern car owner whose details had been forged originally.

Opposite page: Patrolling the streets
Left: The *camorra* managed the street tobacco trade

Gardens and Parks

In a city as dense as this one, there is little room for green space. Most of Naples' public parks will be found outside of the Centro Storico – largely due to the fact that the original city walls insured that public gardens were an impossibility in a place that required every square inch for human habitation. Be warned – the lack of greenery means that many of Naples' fine public grounds are packed solid on sunny days and weekends.

Orto Botanico

Orto Botanico (Botanical Gardens)

Founded by Joseph Bonaparte in 1807, these gardens, while located in one of Naples' most crowded districts, are a haven of peace and tranquillity. The selection of trees and plants is serviceable, including a number of palms, ferns and aquatic shrubs. A *castello* in the centre of the park features museum displays dedicated to the world of botany and is now operated by the Naples University science department. *Via Foria 223. Tel: (081) 449 759. www.ortobotanico.unina.it. Open: By appointment only Mon–Fri 9am–2pm. Metro Cavour or Museo. Bus 14, 15, 47, CD, CS, C51.*

Parco di Capodimonte

The extensive parkland surrounding the highly-recommended Museo di Capodimonte was originally intended for use as hunting grounds for Carlo III. Today, hunting of a different form is in operation in this much-used green lung of the city – that of the opposite sex. For the best city views, go to the southern tip of the grounds past the Museo.

Porta Grande Via Capodimonte. Open: daily 8am–1hr before sunset. Bus 24, 110, R4.

Parco Virgiliano

Amidst the smog-choked streets of traffic lies this little jewel of greenery. To locate it, look under the railway bridge to the left of the church of Santa Maria di Piedigrotte. Climb the long staircase for a look into the **Crypta Neapolitana**, a 1st-century Roman road tunnel – and one of the world's longest. This engineering marvel originally connected Naples to the towns of Pozzuoli and Baia. Due to the precarious condition and old age of the crumbling tunnel, going inside is absolutely forbidden – you will have to make do with a view from above.

At the top of the staircase stands **Virgil's Tomb**. It is unknown whether or not the famed poet is actually buried in this large, beehive-shaped structure, but you shouldn't voice this doubt to any locals.

Salita della Grotta 20, Mergellina. Tel: (081) 669 390. Open: daily

9am–1hr before sunset. Metro Mergellina. Bus C16, C24.

Villa Comunale

Naples' green heart lies here along the edge of the Bay of Naples. Here is where countless Neapolitan couples have flirted and fallen in love, families come to picnic in the sunshine and pensioners choose to take their daily constitutional. Designed as a private park by Luigi Vanvitelli, it was originally used exclusively by the royal family – and it was just opened once a year to the general public on the feast of Mary's Nativity (8 September). Long rather than wide, its grounds follow the Chiaia coastline; however, it is separated from the peace and tranquillity of the lapping waves by the busy Via Francesco Caracciolo.

Riviera di Chiaia. Open: daily May–Oct 7am–midnight; Nov–Apr 7am–10pm. Bus 140, 152, C28, R3. Tram 1.

Museo di Capodimonte

Walk: The Port and University

While not the most picturesque part of Naples, this walk explores the city's nautical traditions and industrial past.
The walk starts at the main entrance of the Stazione Centrale on Piazza Garibaldi.
Allow 3 hours.

1 Stazione Centrale
The main railway station of Naples, this 1960s-constructed monstrosity is heavy on function and light on form. It's interesting only if you like to watch the sea of humanity pass through its doors and onto the transportation and population hub that is the **Piazza Garibaldi** located directly in front of the main doors.
Cross to the far side of Piazza Garibaldi. Proceed down Via P.S. Mancini, and turn left on Via Capuana Maddalena. Then go right down Via Dell'Annunziata. The Santissima Annunziata will be on your left-hand side.

The Port of Naples

2 Santissima Annunziata
(See p45 for details) Via dell'Annunziata 34. Tel: (081) 207 455. Open: Wheel Mon–Sat 9am–1pm. Church closed for restoration.
Continue along the Via Dell'Annunziata until you reach Via Egiziaca a Forcella.

3 The Forcella District
The heart of gangland Naples, this gloomy quarter is the legendary home to the city's lowlife. Honour and poverty combine in this neighbourhood made famous for its gangland connections and petty crime. Safe to explore by day, it's a fascinating glimpse into the lives led by citizens thriving precariously on the edge in one of Europe's richest nations.
Take an immediate left onto Via Pietro Colletta. Continue until you reach Corso Umberto I, and turn right.

4 Corso Umberto I
One of Naples' main thoroughfares, Corso Umberto I is the traffic-clogged artery linking Piazza Garibaldi with the decidedly more attractive trappings of Chiaia and Royal Naples. Originally intended as a cholera break to relieve the city of its problems with plague and disease, Corso Umberto I passes through

some of Naples' poorest communities.
Walk along Corso Umberto I for
approximately 7 blocks. Turn right on
Via Tari and continue until the name
changes to Via G. Paladino.

5 Università

Founded in 1224, Naples University (or
the Università di Napoli Federico II, as it is
officially named) is one of Europe's oldest
and largest. While its faculties are scattered
throughout the city, its traditional heart
lies in Piazza Bovio.
Turn left onto tiny Via G. Orilia and take
another immediate left on Via
Mezzocannone.

6 Musei Inter-dipartimenti

(See p46 for details) Via Mezzocannone 8.
Tel: (081) 253 7516. www.musei.unina.it.
Open: Mon 9am–1.30pm, 3–5pm;
Tue–Fri 9am–1.30pm; Sat, Sun
9am–1pm. Admission charge.
Continue along Via Mezzocannone. The
name will change to Via Pta Di Massa.
Turn onto Via Nuova Marina. Molo
Beverello is on your right.

Fishermen at Lungomare

7 The Port of Naples and Molo Beverello

It may not be pretty, but the busy Port
of Naples is probably the best slice-of-
life segment of the city, providing some
of its most fascinating people-watching
opportunities. Time your visit to
coincide with the early morning or late
evening in order to see the boats going
out or coming in for the day. For the
perfect ending to this stroll, get on
board a ferry departing from the Molo
Beverello for an incomparable view of
the city – preferably at sunset.

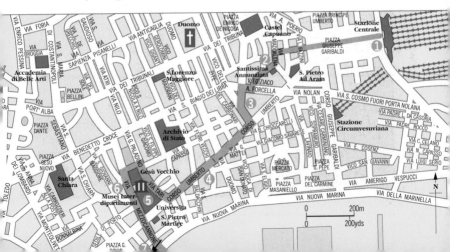

In 1889, the district of Vomero became a viable residential quarter, thanks largely to the invention of a pair of local engineers, Bruno and Ferraro. These two canny industrial pioneers designed a funicular rail system that allowed passengers to ascend the precarious sides of Vomero hill along the Chiaia and Montesanto slopes. The 'train of delights', as it was called, passed up the rural hillside to the top of Vomero, finally stopping to allow passengers a stunning view of the bay. In those days Vomero was known for its vineyards and farmlands – and not for the upmarket apartment blocks of today. Following its successful inclusion into the Neapolitan transport network, locals flocked to the cooler breezes, ample space and altogether more pleasant air of Vomero,

transforming it almost overnight into one of the city's most popular middle-class residential neighbourhoods.

In total, four lines run between Vomero and the districts below: the Chiaia line (1889), Montesanto (1891), the Mergellina and the Centrale (1928). The longest funicular of the four, the Centrale, begins its journey in Via Toledo, reaching a point near the Via Scarlatti halfway between the Chiaia and Montesanto lines. For direct access to the seafront and the western suburbs, the Mergellina funicular, running from Via Manzoni, is the best option.

Rides on the funicular proved to be so popular that a famous song was composed in the late 19th century, broadcasting its reputation. *Funiculì,*

Funiculà can still be heard on many recordings today, especially in the streets of the city that sparked the craze.

As only two trains run on the railway system at any given time (one up and one down), rides can get exceedingly busy during the traditional morning and evening rush hours. It's best to avoid this time of day unless you like the idea of being jammed into the corner of a sweaty train-car leaning on a steep incline. Due to the popularity of casual rides, the usual 90-minute ticket is only useable once on the funicular system.

Before the advent of the funicular age, travellers to Vomero were forced to traverse a long flight of steps leading up from the city centre. By day, these steps make for an enjoyable journey, especially if you want to avoid the chaotic traffic that plagues the city. By night, its location makes it a prime target for muggings, and petty theft. Be alert if you take the risk.

Another funicular railway built by the dynamic design duo of Bruno and Ferraro was a precarious track up the sides of Vesuvius. Erected in 1880, this funicular, consisting of just two cars, took

visitors up to an altitude of 1,180m (3,870ft) above sea level. A number of accidents plagued the system for the duration of its all-too-brief lifetime, finally forcing the Vesuvius funicular to close in 1944.

Tickets can be bought at any of the funicular railway stations. Tel: (081) 763 2519. Trains run every 10 minutes. Funiculare Centrale. From city centre to the Villa Floridiana. Open: daily 6am–1am. Funiculare di Chiaia. From Via del Parco Margherita to the Villa Floridiana. Open: Mon–Thur 7am–10pm; Fri–Sun 7am–1am. Funiculare di Montesanto. Cumana station to the Castel Sant'Elmo and Via Scarlatti. Open: daily 7am–10pm. Funiculare di Mergellina. From Via Mergellina to Via Manzoni. Open: daily 7am–10pm.

Opposite and below: Funicular rides are very popular in Naples

Royal Naples and Monte Echia

If you like centres of royal domination, ancient history, rambling fishermen's quarters and lands stained by the blood of conquering forces, then Royal Naples is the district to explore. The site of Neapolitan power and government since the day the city was founded over 2,500 years ago, Royal Naples is home to more regal tourist treasures than any other part of town.

Fishing is a way of life in parts of Naples

Legends and lore

Legend has it that a group of sailors discovered the body of the siren Parthenope washed up on the rocks at this point on the Campanian coastline. Distraught after having her affections turned down by Ulysses, the mermaid drowned herself, only to have her corpse drift back to shore. In an act of charity, the sailors decided to bury her body on the rock, and thus gave the name of Parthenope (or Paleopolis) to the original settlement.

The development of the city of Naples occurred after the Greeks, who settled on the islands of Megaris and Monte Echia – where Castel dell'Ovo still sits – decided to move inland to form a new town or 'Neapolis'.

Monte Echia

The home of ancient Paleopolis sits above the crater rim of an extinct volcano. Located southwest of Piazza Plebiscito, Monte Echia is the oldest section of the city, dating back to the days when this tiny dot-on-the-map was just an unimportant settlement on the edge of the Greek Empire. The end of the Greek age and the success of the Roman Empire proved to be a boom for Paleopolis – by this time renamed Neapolis – as famous citizens from the capital were drawn to the area's natural beauty and healing waters. In the 1st century BC, the great Roman general Lucullus owned much of Monte Echia, building an extensive villa complex that stretched from the shoreline across as far as Mergellina.

Military might

Monte Echia's military connections remain strong – both the police headquarters and a military academy look out over this cradle of western civilisation. Views of the bay, while obstructed, can still be enjoyed from the terrace of a decidedly run-down garden at the top of the hill just off Salita Echia.

La Nunziatella

Visit this tiny Baroque church to understand the saying 'size isn't everything'. Built for the Bourbon royal family in 1787, La Nunziatella features a beautiful marble altar and uniquely tiled flooring. Today the church is owned and used by the military academy located next door.

Via Generale Parisi 16.
Tel: (081) 764 1451. Open: Sun 9–10am for mass. All other times by appointment. Bus C22.

Pizzofalcone

For beautiful views and a distinctive 'olde-worlde' buzz, the Pizzofalcone district is the place for you. Two churches serve the community, **Santa Maria degli Angeli** and **Santa Egiziaca a Pizzofalcone**, but neither is of any specific significance. Santa Maria boasts a massive dome – although you won't be able to see it from the road. Santa Egiziaca is known for its unique convex façade.

Down by the seaside

Castel dell'Ovo is reached by zigzagging your way down Mount Echia via the rambling **Rampa di Pizzofalcone**. From the bottom of the curving walkway, Via Partenope thrusts left towards the Santa Lucia fishermen's quarter and right to the five-star trappings of Chiaia. To find your way back to the Piazza del Plebiscito, follow Via Partenope along the seafront. The **Fontana dell'Immacolatella**, designed by Pietro Bernini and Michelangelo Naccherino, sits halfway along the journey back to the city centre.

Santa Lucia

Featuring some of Naples' most picturesque back-alleys and hidden streets, the rambling fishermen's quarter of Pallonetto in Santa Lucia is a cosy corner of the city which is perfect for getting lost in. Filled with charming urban views, Santa Lucia has few tourist-geared sites that warrant a visit. Instead, enjoy a stroll along Via Chiatamone and Via Santa Lucia to take in the area's attractions.

King of Naples, Palazzo Reale

Royal Naples

Filled with piazzas and palazzi, this traffic-free district is packed with royal relics and elegant shopping. Important buildings range in size from the huge to the absolutely enormous, in keeping with the egos of the residents who originally called this corner of the city home – the Neapolitan royal families.

Piazza Plebiscito

Acquedotto Carmigiano

Naples' most intriguing tour takes you underground and through the various tunnels, cisterns and wells that make up the city's water system. The *Carmigiano* drainage system was designed and built during the 16th- and 17th-century reign of the Spanish viceroys. Naples' population was expanding at a massive rate, and a method was needed to bring constant supplies of fresh water to newly expanded districts.

Hour-long tours take you to 40m (130ft) below the city centre, past alcoves used as air-raid shelters in World War II. This is definitely not an experience for the claustrophobic!
Vico Sant'Anna di Palazzo 52. Tel: (081) 400 256. Open: Guided tours depart from Bar Gambrinus, Via Chiaia 1–2. Thur 9pm; Sat 10am, noon, 6pm; Sun 10am, 11am, noon, 6pm. Bus 24, C22, C82, R2, R3.

Galleria Umberto

A vaulted glass and steel-covered shopping arcade similar in style and design to the Galleria in Milan, this indoor wallet-busting mall is packed with a number of upmarket boutiques catering to the tourist trade. Today, renovations are much-needed to replace a number of missing glass panes. Not recommended if you are trying to escape the rain – the ceiling allows in almost as much water as a power shower!
From Piazza Trieste e Trento to Via Toledo. Bus 24, C22, C82, R2, R3.

Piazza Plebiscito

On hot summer weekends and New Year's Eve, this glorious public square is the site of music concerts, open-air theatre, buskers and political rallies. It's hard to believe that the restored volcanic cobblestones were covered in grime and the exhaust fumes of hundreds of inner-city buses as recently as 1994. Surrounding the piazza are Doric columns and a series of bronze equestrian statues dedicated to kings of the Bourbon dynasty.

San Francesco di Paola

An unpopular local church defaced by graffiti and generations of pigeon detritus, the neoclassical design of San Francesco is surprisingly rare in this city of Baroque ostentation. Its location on the Piazza Plebiscito provides its doors with a stream of visitors drawn by its size and 53m (175ft)-high dome.

Piazza Plebiscito. Tel: (081) 764 5133. Open: Mon–Sat 8am–noon, 3.30–6pm; Sun 8am–1pm. Bus 24, C22, C82, R2, R3.

The roof of the Galleria Umberto I

Walk: The Birth of a City

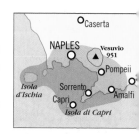

Explore the earliest years of Naples in this walk, taking you from the sandy shores of the Bay of Naples to the city's royal seats of power.

The walk starts at the main entrance of the Castel dell'Ovo and takes approximately 3 hours.

1 Castel dell'Ovo

(See p38 for details) Via Partenope. Tel: (081) 246 4111. Open: Mon–Sat 9am–6pm; Sun 9am–1.30pm. From the main entrance, go straight on until you reach Via Partenope. Turn right and then take an immediate left onto Via Santa Lucia.

2 Santa Lucia

This maze-like quarter has been home to the fishermen of the city for countless generations. Getting lost in these streets is a treat, especially if you enjoy

It's easy to get lost in the narrow streets

watching everyday Neapolitan street life and the people who take part in it. If you like fresh fish, then a meal at any of the restaurants in the area is highly recommended.

Continue along Via Santa Lucia. At the end of the street lies Via Console. Cross the green space and the other road running parallel to Via Console (Via Acton) to reach your next stop on the itinerary.

3 Giardini Pubblici

These public gardens aren't the best in the city, but they are a favourite spot for courting couples and troubled teens. On weekends and pleasant evenings, this small park is covered with excitable groups of the pubescent and pre-pubescent hoping to practise their flirtation skills with members of the opposite sex. The views of the Bay are quite special, and it's a nice place to enjoy a quick drink or picnic lunch if you are so inclined – many others are.

With your back to the gardens, continue going right up Via Acton.

4 Palazzo Reale

(See p40 for details) Piazza del Plebiscito. Tel: (081) 794 4021. Open: Mon, Tue, Thur–Sun 9am–8pm; ticket office closes 1hr earlier. Admission charge.

5 Piazza Plebiscito
(See p64 for details)

6 Gambrinus Café
The watering hole of choice for the
Neapolitan élite and their favoured
artists, the Gambrinus has been dishing
up mouthwatering cakes and positively
passionate pastries for over a century.
Its location near the doors of both
the Teatro San Carlo and the Galleria
Umberto makes it the ideal post-
shopping and pre-show location for
either a quick coffee or a long gossip.
Some of the rooms have only just been
reopened after the Fascist leadership
of the 1930s closed them down for

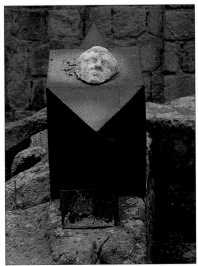

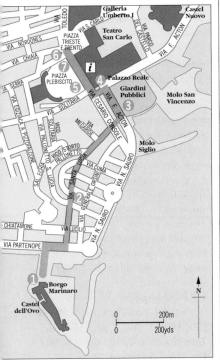

The city walls

their suspected links with left-wing
politicians. Today, you are unlikely
to spot any reds in the place unless
seen as part of a motif in a Hermès
headscarf. To get one of the better
tables, be sure to dress as smartly as
possible, making sure that all designer
labels are coolly conspicuous. These
waiters can sniff new money and/or a
tourist better than a bloodhound!
Via Chiaia 1–2. Tel: (081) 417 582.
Open: daily 8am–1.30am.
*Depart from the Gambrinus entrance to
your next and final destination.*

7 Acquedotto Carmigiano
*(See p64 for details) Vico Sant'Anna
di Palazzo 52. Tel: (081) 400 256.*
*Open: Guided tours depart from Bar
Gambrinus, Via Chiaia 1–2. Thur 9pm;
Sat 10am, noon, 6pm; Sun 10am, 11am,
noon, 6pm.*

Piazza Cavour

Catacombs and Craniums

While imagery relating to bones, skulls and death is nothing new in a town as dedicated to the Gothic as Naples is, there is something decidedly eerie – and yet oh so captivating – about the high number of catacombs and cemeteries available for public inspection. If you're of a delicate nature, don't worry too much about what you'll find on your subterranean tour – it's an absolutely 'deadly' experience worth exploring.

Catacombe di San Gaudiso
Location of a burial site that has been used since the 5th century AD, this extensive subterranean collection of catacombs holds the remains of St Gaudiosus, a 5th-century North African bishop. His burial here transformed the labyrinthine, subterranean graveyard into an important shrine and place of holy pilgrimage. A variety of fascinating ancient burial practices is displayed and outlined by the competent tour guides, who lead you through the dark and musty caves that weave through the volcanic rock. Hour-long tours depart from the church of Santa Maria alla Sanità situated directly above the catacombs.
Via della Sanità. Tel: (081) 544 1305.
Open: Guided tours daily 9.30am,
10.15am, 11am, 11.45am, 12.30pm, plus
Sat 5.10pm, 5.50pm, 6.30pm. Admission
charge. Metro Cavour or Museo. Bus C51,
C52.

Catacombe di San Gennaro
Lucky San Gennaro. Not only does he have a city in his thrall over two phials of his blood, he also gets to commune with the dead in a catacomb named after him. Two levels of catacombs contain some much-muddied frescoes dating as far back as the 2nd century AD. But it wasn't until the body of San Gennaro was brought here in the 5th century that the catacombs became a place of pilgrimage and religious worship.
Via Capodimonte 16. Tel: (081) 741 1071.
Open: Guided tours daily 9.30am,
10.15am, 11am, 11.45am. Group tours
available by appointment only. Admission
charge. Bus 24, 110, R4.

Catacombe di San Severo
Named after Saint Severus, these catacombs lost their importance when the remains of its namesake were moved to the church of San Giorgio Maggiore in the 9th century. Go to see the wonderful 4th-century frescoes of St Peter and St Paul – the first representations of the apostles anywhere in the city.
Piazzetta San Severo a Capodimonte 81.
Tel: (081) 544 1305. Open: Church

San Vincenzo, Santa Maria alla Sanità

Mon–Fri 9.30–11.30am, 5.30–7.30pm; Sat 5.30–7.30pm; Sun 9.30–11.30am. Catacombs by appointment only. Donations expected. Metro Cavour or Museo. Bus C51, C52.

Cimitero delle Fontanelle

Closed to the public since the 1970s, this cemetery has an extremely grim history, due to the number of dead transported here after the cholera epidemic of 1835. Eager to remove the diseased deceased from locations inside the city walls, hundreds of bodies were buried here in mass anonymous graves. When cholera reared its ugly head once again in 1974, more bodies were dumped in an effort to stem the tide of the disease. Over 40,000 skulls and bones are now stacked up throughout the massive cavern that makes up the structure. During World War II, 'skull worshipping' became a popular fad, as parents of children killed in action would adopt skulls in memory of their sons. *Via delle Fontanelle 154. Tel: (081) 296 944. Closed indefinitely. Check with the Napoli Sotterranea society regarding potential reopening plans. Metro Cavour or Museo. Bus C51.*

Walk: Via Toledo's Faded Grandeur

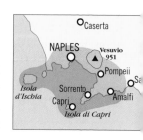

The history of Naples is one of permanent destruction and regeneration. As each period of fame and fortune fell by the wayside, residents shrugged off their problems, certain that the next period of good luck was sure to be just around the corner – at least in a few hundred years or so. In this walk we explore the grand palazzi of the Via Toledo, built during the boom years of the 18th century. They may have lost a bit of their lustre, but they'll never completely lose their looks.

This walk starts at the Galleria Umberto and takes approximately 2 hours.

1 Galleria Umberto
(See p64 for details) The complex runs from Piazza Trieste e Trento to Via Toledo. With your back to the Via Toledo exit, turn right up Via Toledo away from the Piazza Plebiscito. Your walk will continue straight on in this direction along the Via Toledo.

2 Palazzo Doria d'Angri
While you can't 'pull an Evita' by visiting the spot yourself, the balcony of this crumbling palazzo marks the location where Giuseppe Garibaldi declared the Unified Kingdom of Italy in September 1860. Note the pockmarks on the walls left from a World War II bomb that almost destroyed the building.
Via Toledo 29.

3 Banco di Napoli
A prime example of imposing 1930s architecture favoured by the Fascist regime. Think cold concrete, combined

with athletic depictions of 'pure-blood' common people, and you get the idea.
Via Toledo 178.

4 Palazzo Zevallos di Stigliano
A typical Via Toledo palazzo, boasting a door designed by Cosimo Fanzago. The building is now a bank.
Via Toledo 184.

La Rinascente, Palazzo Buono

5 Palazzo Barbaja

Famous more for its residents than its design, this palazzo was the home of opera composer Gioacchino Rossini (*The Barber of Seville*) for seven years in the early 19th century.
Via Toledo 205.

6 Palazzo Berio

This palazzo was designed by noted architect Luigi Vanvitelli, who is famous for having also designed the Villa Comunale and the Reggia in Caserta. The main square of Vomero is named after this favourite son of the city.
Via Toledo 256.

7 Palazzo Buono

Once one of the largest privately-owned palazzi on the street, the Palazzo Buono is now owned by the Rinascente department store. While the interiors have been completely gutted in order

Palazzo Doria

to open up the floors for large-scale shopping, this is one of the best opportunities you'll have to actually go inside one of the grand dames of design. In keeping with the salacious past of Neapolitan noble classes who frequented this home, La Rinascente is renowned for its selection of underwear and perfumes.
Via Toledo 340. Tel: (081) 411 511.
Open: Mon–Sat 9am–8pm; Sun 10am–2pm, 5–8pm.
Continue along Via Toledo past Piazza Dante. The name changes to Via E. Pessina.

8 The Museo Nazionale Archeologico

(See p36 for details) Piazza Museo Archeologico, Piazza Museo 19. Tel: (081) 564 8941. www.archeona.arti.beniculturali.it. Open: Museum Mon, Wed–Sun 9am–7.30pm; ticket office closes 1hr earlier. Gabinetto segreto Mon, Wed–Sun 9.30am–1.30pm, 2.30–6.30pm. Guided tours every 30 min. Admission charge.

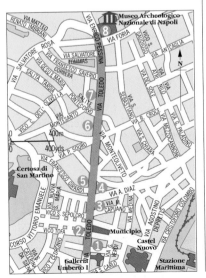

Capodimonte

Visit the glorious hillside heaven of Capodimonte if you're a fan of breathtaking museums, lush gardens, vivid views and other tantalising touristy treats perfect for those days when you're weary or just plain worn out.

The Art Card gives you free museum entry

On a clear day you can see forever from the balconies of the Palazzo Reale di Capodimonte (*see p40*) – built for King Charles III in the 18th century. Before the construction of this massive pile, Capodimonte was a generally disregarded hill located far outside the city walls. But it was the king's passion for sport that changed all of that. This verdant retreat provided top-class hunting grounds, perfect for those typically overcast Neapolitan days when there was just nothing for a king to do.

A Garden of Eden

While it's not even a quarter of the size of Europe's grandest green spaces (*Bois de Boulogne, Hyde Park, Tiergarten*), the park surrounding the **Museo di Capodimonte** can lay claim to being one of the best on the continent. Designed in the 18th century by Ferdinand Sanfelice, the park has five avenues radiating from the palace like spokes on a wheel.

What lies beneath

The rest of the sights of Capodimonte are downhill from here – literally. Directly below the palazzo lie the remains of what was once the most important point of pilgrimage in the city of Naples. The **Catacombe di San Gennaro** (*see p68*), once held relics of the city's patron saint San Gennaro. When his remains and phials of his blood were moved to the **Duomo**, the catacombs lost their page in Neapolitan history books.

Osservatorio astronomico

From below the ground to above the stars, the astronomical observatory was built in 1819 in order to take advantage of the clear views from the top of one of Naples' highest points. King Ferdinand I built this neoclassical structure soon after recapturing his lost throne. Check out the collection of equipment, both historic and modern, in one of Europe's first observatories of its kind. During the tour there are occasional opportunities to try out some of the tools of the trade, depending on the mood of your guide – so be sure to smile a lot and keep opinions to yourselves.

Salita Moiariello 16. Tel: (081) 557 5111. www.na.astro.it. Open: Guided tours only, held approximately once a month. Book well in advance by phone: Mon–Fri 8–10am. Bus 24, 110, R4.

ALL WALLED OUT

There must be more than one way around a set of city walls. At least that's what Byzantine General Belisarius had to figure out during his siege of Naples in AD 536. Deciding to avoid the futility of a direct attack, the knowledgeable General used the city's defences against them by sneaking through the **Ponti Rossi** aqueduct. This fresh-water supplier, built by the Emperor Claudius in the 1st century, provided direct access into the heart of the city centre. You can still see the well-preserved ruins of the aqueduct leading down from Capodimonte's **Porta Grande**. Not only was the General victorious, he also managed to avoid an almost certain watery grave.

Porcelain display at Capodimonte

Vomero

Before World War II, Vomero was seen as a small, countrified suburb of sprawling Naples. Families would take the funicular up the hillside past the numerous farms (the district officially had a higher population of sheep than it did of people) and enjoy picnics in the cool air of the **Castel Sant'Elmo** (*see p40*).

Cloister of San Martino

With postwar reconstruction came postwar gloom as unscrupulous property speculators transformed the district into a sea of middle-class high-rise developments almost overnight. For years afterwards, Vomero was seen as the worst neighbourhood in Naples in terms of traffic chaos. With only four funicular lines running every ten minutes between Vomero and the city centre, commuting was a mess. Only with the introduction of the underground station and new metro lines has any headway even started to be made in what was essentially Europe's largest permanent parking lot.

Via Scarlatti
At the heart of the community lies Via Scarlatti – recently pedestrianised in order to promote the new car-free community Vomero is so desperately trying to invoke. Café tables pour out onto this elegant tree-lined avenue, bringing out thousands of locals on warm summer nights. A stroll down here rivals that even of glamorous Via Toledo amongst the upper classes of Neapolitan society. The focal point of Via Scarlatti is Piazza Vanvitelli, named after the local architect who made his

name designing such structures as the Villa Comunale and the Reggia in Caserta.

Parco della Floridiana
If the tree-lined avenue of Via Scarlatti doesn't calm your nerves, then this favoured park most probably will. Built as a wedding gift for the Duchess of Floridiana by her husband King Ferdinand, the gardens and villa were opened to the public in the 1920s after they were purchased by the state. Since that time, the system of paths and intimate benches has made it one of the best spots for a quiet stroll in the city. *Via Cimarosa 77. Tel: (081) 578 1776. Open: Park daily 8.30am–1hr before sunset. Funicular Montesanto to Via Morghen, Centrale to Piazzetta Fuga or Chiaia to Via Cimarosa. Bus E4, V1.*

Corso Vittorio Emanuele
Each district of Naples has its 'main street' and Vomero is no exception. Corso Vittorio Emanuele wraps around the length of Vomero, separating it from the streets of the city centre below. In certain sections, it's decidedly ugly. However, the bulk of Naples' luxury hotel options are situated along this

avenue on the border with Chiaia. Why Vomero, you might ask? The answer is the views. Clinging precariously to the hillside above, residents of this tiny stretch of land enjoy the cooling breezes that come with living halfway up the inner city's highest point in addition to some of the most stunningly unobstructed views of the Bay of Naples below. A drink at the **Grand Hotel Parker's** (*Corso Vittorio Emanuele 135*), while enjoying the sunset, was almost a rite of passage for 'Grand Tour' British tourists during the peak of 19th-century travel to the city. Just watch your feet while walking down the street – Corso Vittorio has more 'doggy-doo' on it than any other street in Naples.

Vista over Naples and Vesuvius from the Castel Sant'Elmo

Walk: Gothic Ghoulishness of Vomero

You may be excused for not knowing the name of Lamont Young (1851–1929). But in Naples, this Neapolitan-born son of British parents was a true hero of neo-Gothic architecture. This eccentric engineer constructed his unconventional edifices on lands purchased immediately below the Villa Floridiana by his father.

In addition to taking you past surviving examples of Young's work, this tour takes in the highlights of the Vomero district. The walk should take approximately 3 hours, beginning at the main entrance of the Museo della Ceramica.

1 Museo della Ceramica
(See p47 for details) Via Cimarosa 77. Tel: (081) 578 1776. Open: Guided tours only. Tue–Sun 9.30am, 11am, 12.30pm. Admission charge. Explore the museum and surrounding park, making sure to take in the views from the southern terrace.

From the terrace, continue south until you reach the Via Parco Grifeo.

2 Parco Grifeo
Lamont Young's family certainly made a good investment when they bought this plot of land surrounding the Rampa Privata al Parco Grifeo from the heirs of

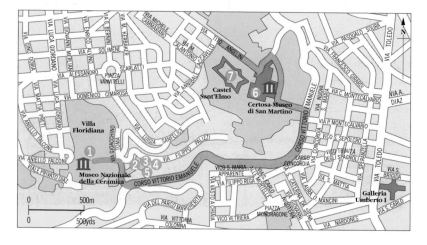

Villa Floridiana

the Duchess Floridiana. After the purchase was completed, the area became the most popular place to see and be seen by the Neapolitan nouveau riche.
Continue downhill along the Via. From the Via, look for the home with the large watchtower.

3 Castello Grifeo

Young's first design, this whimsically fancy residence was inspired by Sir Walter Scott's Castle in Abbotsford, England, built in 1820. Authenticity was maintained right down to the last detail, including fake cracks built right into the walls. Unfortunately, you can't enter this fantastic creation as it is privately owned.
Parco Grifeo 37.
Look next door for the next stop.

4 Palazzina Grifeo

In contrast to his first flight of fancy, Young's second design was strictly neo-Renaissance in tone – although you'd never guess it by looking at it. Sweeping changes to the exteriors have obliterated many of the original features from this privately owned – and thus impossible to enter – home.
Parco Grifeo 39.
Continue downhill to the Corso Vittorio Emanuele. Turn left onto the Corso.

5 Castello Aselmeyer

Tudor style comes to Naples in this out-of-place residence suspended on the hillside overlooking Corso Vittorio Emanuele. In addition to the usual bow windows and verandas so popular in Tudor architecture, Young incorporated Gothic elements in the design of the home, including a pair of gargoyles that clash intriguingly with the rest of the building.
Corso Vittorio Emanuele 166.
Follow the Corso until you reach a church on the left-hand side. A series of staircases going uphill should be to the right of it. Follow these stairs, and when you reach the top, turn right and follow the street around until you reach the Certosa-Museo di San Martino.

6 Certosa-Museo di San Martino

(See p46 for details) Largo San Martino 5. Tel/Fax: (081) 578 1769. Open: Tue–Sat 8.30am–7.30pm; Sun 9am–7.30pm. Admission charge.
Go north along the Via Tito Angelini. Castel Sant'Elmo will be on your left.

7 Castel Sant'Elmo

(See p40 for details) Via Tito Angelini 22. Tel: (081) 578 4030. Open: Tue–Sun 9am–7.30pm (ticket office closes 1hr earlier). Admission charge.

The roof of Castel Sant'Elmo

Walk: A Sensual Seafront Stroll

This walk along the Bay of Naples is a particular favourite for locals on a sunny Sunday afternoon. You can still spot the remains of the pine-wooded hills and fragrant backdrops that intoxicated visitors here in the 19th century during the era of the Grand European tour. Follow in the footsteps of travellers past and present on this walk, taking you from the heart of the city into the idyllic neighbourhoods of Mergellina and the western suburbs.

Beginning at the grandstand in the Villa Comunale, this walk takes 2 hours to complete.

1 Villa Comunale

(See p57 for details) Riviera di Chiaia. Open: May–Oct daily 7am–midnight. Nov–Apr daily 7am–10pm.

2 Stazione Zoologica (Acquaria)

Situated in the centre of the Villa Comunale, this is one of Europe's oldest aquariums, founded in 1872 by German naturalist Anton Dohrn. The original 24 tanks still stand, calling themselves

View of Posillipo

home to a number of local aquatic species, including octopuses, lobsters, seahorses and various fish. Legend has it that the liberating forces of 1944 held a victory banquet in the aquarium featuring a menu of its entire edible population.

Villa Comunale. Tel: (081) 583 3111. Open: Tue–Sat 9am–6pm, Sun 9.30am–7pm. Admission charge. Cross the Riviera di Chiaia to reach your next stop, the Villa Pignatelli.

3 Villa Pignatelli

This 19th-century villa has a strong British connection. Ferdinand Acton, son of the British prime minister Sir John Acton, built this imposing residence complete with a beautiful English-style garden. Eventually purchased and remodelled by the Rothschild family, the villa and grounds fell into the hands of the Italian government in 1952. Inside are some fantastic porcelains, busts and

The bandstand at Villa Comunale

landscapes, which are well worth exploring. Villa Pignatelli's crown jewel is the 17th-century painting of *St George* by Francesco Guarino, although this is by no means the only masterpiece worth checking out. Fans of landscapes should make a beeline for the wonderful collection of 17th- and 18th-century works in Room six.

Riviera di Chiaia 200. Tel: (081) 669 675. Open: Tue–Sun 9am–2pm. Admission charge.

Follow the Riviera until it reaches a fork. Take Via Mergellina on the left.

4 The Chalets

A rewarding avenue running along the bay, Via Mergellina takes you directly to the Chalets – named after the purpose-built ice-cream huts and restaurants that line the route. This is a popular late-evening hot spot for a quick bite or a night on the tiles.

The Chalets are at the end of Via Mergellina on the way to Posillipo. Should you not be ready for a break and a bite, stop under the railway tracks to explore the Parco Virgiliano.

5 Santa Maria di Piedigrotta

Sitting under the railway bridge is this seemingly unprepossessing church. Once the focal point of an exciting song festival celebrated on the feast-day celebrations of Mary's Nativity (8 September), efforts are being made to bring back the musical tradition sometime in the near future.

Open: Mon–Sat 7am–noon, 5–8pm; Sun 7am–2pm, 5–8pm.

6 Parco Virgiliano

(See p56 for details) Salita della Grotta 20, Mergellina. Tel: (081) 669 390. Open: daily 9am–1hr before sunset.

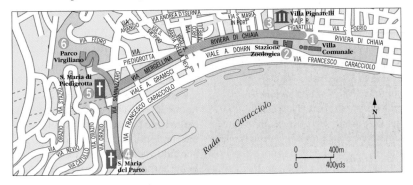

Pompeii, Herculaneum and Vesuvius

A visit to the towns that lie at the base of Vesuvius has been an integral part of a European's 'Grand Tour' education ever since the remains of the Roman town of Herculaneum were discovered in 1710. 'Yobbo' youths of yesteryear followed in the moneyed footsteps of millionaires from long ago by embarking on an extended stay to the region as part of their classical education – necessary for a respected position in the civil service or at royal court.

Temple of Apollo, Pompeii

Today, a trip to Pompeii, Herculaneum and Vesuvius is less an educational stay and more a packed historical day trip away from the hustle and bustle of Naples. Considering the manner in which the treasures of the area were plundered by the Bourbons three centuries ago, excavations are surprisingly complete. While a knowledgeable archaeologist will shudder at the sight of primitive tunnelling techniques used in some of the oldest digs, the buildings and layout that remain give a surprisingly complete account of what life was probably like in the area almost 2,000 years ago.

Above the excavated sites and ancient homes lies one of Europe's most poverty stricken communities. The stretch of Campanian coastline running from Portici to Stabia has some of the continent's highest unemployment rates and a level of urban blight and depression to match. A ride along the Circumvesuviana train line from Naples to your final destination is not a classic journey in any sense of the word.

Graffiti-covered stations and crumbling apartment blocks testify to the area's long period of decline.

Rising above all the history and heartache is the symbol of Naples, towering Mount Vesuvius. While a constant plume of smoke no longer runs from this volcanic juggernaut, it is by no means dormant. Its last eruption in 1944 was extremely destructive, obliterating thousands of homes and heaping even greater problems on a population already distraught by the damage of World War II. Haphazard rebuilding has replaced everything that was lost in the postwar eruption; however, you can still see abandoned lava fields only a few miles away from densely populated communities.

With 1.5 million visitors arriving in Pompeii every year, the cost of maintenance and the demands for a tourist infrastructure are the greatest challenges of the area. Large-scale European Union developments are pumping money into the vicinity; however there is a heavy push for

Public fountain, Pompeii

increased privatisation in order to help cut costs in the cash-strapped Italian cultural heritage ministry. Plans are afoot to transform formerly 'lesser' excavations – such as those at Stabiae – into more popular destinations, with the aim of diverting the high tourist numbers away from Pompeii and into other communities in the region. Until an equivalent amount of investment money is pumped away from the usual two key archaeological sights (Herculaneum and Pompeii), this goal will remain just a pipe dream. Pompeii and Herculaneum remain the star UNESCO World Heritage Sites of the region and are well worth hours, if not days, of dedicated time to explore their hidden corners and walls of wonder.

The Basics of Pompeii

On 24 August, AD 79, Vesuvius unleashed a sea of lava, ash and sulphurous gas onto the unsuspecting residents of the various towns and villages that dotted the base of the not-so-dormant volcano. Pompeii, the largest populated area other than Naples on the Campanian coastline, received the brunt of Vesuvius' hellish destruction. Luckily, modern-day archaeologists have two letters penned by Pliny the Younger, describing the violence of the eruption, with which they can develop modern-day conclusions as to the minute-by-minute effects of the eruption.

The Forum

While Pompeii was a traditional holiday home for the rich and powerful of Rome, it had lost much of its popularity by the time Vesuvius decided to flatten it. Had the volcano decided to erupt a mere century earlier, half of Rome's elite and many of its most powerful leaders would have been killed. The rapid destruction of the town is perhaps best understood by looking at the plaster 'statues' cast from the reliefs left by bodies in the now-hardened volcanic mud. The finest examples are located on the top floor of the Museo Nazionale Archeologico in Naples.

As Pompeii is such a widely-visited tourist destination and a UNESCO World Heritage Site, getting there is extremely easy – if sometimes a little crowded. SITA (*tel: (081) 552 2176*) runs frequent bus services from Via Pisanelli in Naples to Pompeii. Look for the stop

located near Piazza Municipio. If you have a rental car, the A3 will drop you right at the doorstep of the ancient town. Take the Pompeii exit from the A3 motorway and follow the stream of automobiles heading in the same direction. However, the traffic chaos of the region may make you think twice about considering either of the above two options. Road travel between Naples and Pompeii will take at least twice as long as you think it will, no matter what time of day you plan your departure. Trains are by far the easiest option. The Circumvesuviana railway (*tel: (081) 772 2444/www.vesuviana.it*) runs frequent services from the Stazione Circumvesuviana, taking about 30–40 minutes. Be sure to get off at Pompeii Scavi-Villa dei Misteri station for direct access to ancient Pompeii. Fares depend

on distance travelled. Your best bet is to get a day pass covering Fascia 3 (Zone 3) between Naples and Pompeii. The cost is €4.03 and covers all your travel, including trips within the city of Naples.

If you plan on visiting a number of the five major archaeological sites (Boscoreale, Herculaneum, Oplontis, Pompeii and Stabiae), save yourself a ton of money by purchasing a cumulative ticket costing €13.50. Tickets are valid for three days and can be purchased at the ticket offices of any of the sites.

Scavi di Pompeii
Via Villa dei Misteri 2. Tel: (081) 536 5154. Open: Apr–Oct daily 8.30am–7.30pm; ticket office closes at 6pm. Nov–Mar daily 8.30am–5pm; ticket office closes at 3.30pm. Admission charge.

The Great Palaestra

Walk: Pompeii in a Day

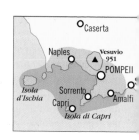

This walk covers the best of Pompeii for those with a limited amount of time. Ideally, a visitor to the area would have weeks to explore its countless hidden corners of splendour, sleepy side streets and examples of everyday ancient Roman life.

Count on spending at least 3 hours on this walk. It begins at the main ticket office.

1 Porta Marina

This gateway to the city (one of seven original gates leading into town) was closest to the sea, thus giving it its name. While the shoreline was once much closer to the town than it is today, a canal is believed to have led from the bay to the town, providing valuable sea access.
Continue straight along the Via Marina.

2 Basilica

Originally Pompeii's court of law, the rectangular buildings with semicircular apses formed the original model for early Christian churches.

Basilica

3 Forum

If Pompeii had a main square of activity, then this would have been it. Surrounding the Forum were the most important buildings of the day, including the court of law, local administrative offices, city archives, the senate house and the seat of the local magistrates.
Continue on the Via di Mercurio away from the Forum. The Tempio di Giove will be on the left with the Macellum directly opposite.

4 Tempio di Giove

Pompeii's most important place of worship, this temple was dedicated to the god Jupiter – chief deity of the Roman religion. Already severely damaged in an earlier earthquake, Vesuvius polished off the rest of the building, leaving little of the original structure standing today.

5 Macellum

This is ancient Pompeii's original meat and fish market. The 12 plinths in the centre of the courtyard once supported posts, which upheld a conical roof. Many bones found in a nearby drain

testify to the covered area's use as a provisions and food source.
Continue straight along the Via di Mercurio.

6 Terme del Foro

If you have the time, skip these baths in favour of the much larger and more extravagant Terme Stabiane later in this walk. If you don't, then skip the out-of-the-way Terme Stabiane and enjoy these tiny baths notable for their original stucco decoration and well-preserved marble fountain.
Turn right on Via di Fortuna and take the first left. The Casa del Fauno will be on the right-hand side.

7 Casa del Fauno

The House of the Faun is one of the largest and most sophisticated in Pompeii. Named after the small bronze statue found in the middle of the marble *impluvium*, the house is

decorated in paintings and mosaics depicting the Battle of Issus in 330 BC between Alexander the Great and the Persian emperor Darius III.
Back-track to the Via di Fortuna and turn right. Follow the Via di Fortuna south until it changes names to the Via di Terme. You will see a Y-junction on the right-hand side. Take the left fork on Via Consolare. Follow this street to the Via dei Sepolcri, then right on the Viale alla Villa dei Misteri.

8 Villa dei Misteri

The Villa of Mysteries has one of the most important decorative and fresco collections in the Roman world. Experts believe that the frescoes lining the *trichlinium* depict a woman's initiation into the cult of Dionysus.
Head south back down Viale alla Villa dei Misteri, and turn left on Via Marina. Continue as it becomes Via dell'Abbondanza until you reach the Terma Stabiane on the left-hand side.

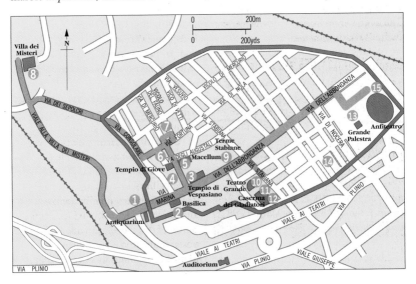

Pompeii fresco

9 Terme Stabiane

The largest collection of baths in ancient Pompeii, featuring an exercise area surrounded by men's and women's bathing sections. The most noteworthy location in the baths is in the stuccoed vault of the men's *apodyterium* (changing room), where you will find finely painted images of nymphs and cupids.

Exit the Terme and turn left. Walk along the road until you reach the train station. This would be a good opportunity to have lunch or a quick drink. Re-enter ancient Pompeii through the Porta Marina and continue straight past the Forum along Via dei Abbondanza. The Teatro Grande will be on your left.

10 Teatro Grande

This stunning theatre, built in the 2nd century BC, was dug out of the slope of the terrain, with a backdrop of the Sarno river plain and the heights of the Monti Lattari.

Turn right onto Via Stabiana. The next 2 sites will be on your right.

11 Odeion/Theatrum Tectum

Pompeii's music concert hall had a capacity of two thousand. This is probably the world's first covered stadium, featuring a permanent roof above the semicircular *cavea* (seating area), which provided welcome shade during the height of the summer season.

12 Casa del Casti Amanti

Work was being done on this house right up until the moment the city was destroyed – most likely to patch up damage from the tremors that had been affecting the areas for days leading up to the eruption. It provides a valuable look into Roman life and the ways it dealt with the shaky situation in 'volcano alley'. As soon as Vesuvius exploded, workers bolted the scene, hastily leaving tools where they lay and plastering unfinished – forever.

Back-track to the Via dell'Abbondanza and continue along the road away from the Porta Marina. The Palaestra will be on the right with the amphitheatre and vineyards either side of it.

13 Palaestra

A rectangular exercise ground dating to Augustinian times. Look for the graffiti left by regular users of the area on the surrounding columns.

14 Vineyards

Vineyards using techniques developed from Ancient Roman methods have been planted using varieties and growth systems from the period. To accomplish this goal, researchers looked at local frescoes in order to determine the plant and fruit species represented. While attempts are being made to produce authentic wine, similar to the vintages of the day, it is thought that the richly scented nose of ancient Roman wines is unlikely to appeal to modern-day palates.

15 Anfiteatro

Small by Roman standards, this amphitheatre could only hold approximately 20,000 spectators. Built in 80 BC, this elliptically-shaped structure was the site for the city's gladiatorial games. It is probably the best-preserved structure of its kind, complete with three sections of seats and a series of *vomitoria* (entrances) at the top. Depending on restoration, the amphitheatre is occasionally closed to visitors.

Fresco at the Garden of Loreius Tiburtinus

The Basics of Herculaneum

In many ways it could be argued that the remains and treasures of Herculaneum are even greater than those at Pompeii. Unfortunately, two millennia of population growth have built-up over the ruins, leaving much of the city buried under a sea of high-rises and concrete.

Triton in Thermae mosaic

Unlike Pompeii, death came painfully slowly to the residents of Herculaneum. Citizens thought they had escaped the worst of the destruction, until heavy rainfall hit Vesuvius, transforming the earth into a sea of mud, lava and ash that hurtled down the mountainsides directly on top of the city. This torrent covered the ancient ground level to a depth of over 20m (65ft), making eventual excavation extremely difficult, while ensuring that the remains were

left in a remarkable state of preservation.

Getting to Herculaneum is even easier than getting to Pompeii as it's situated under the city of Ercolano, approximately halfway between Naples' Stazione Centrale and Pompeii. Once again, driving to Herculaneum is ill-advised, due to the traffic that plagues the roads of the Campanian coastline. If you must get behind the wheel of a car, follow the A3 motorway to Ercolano

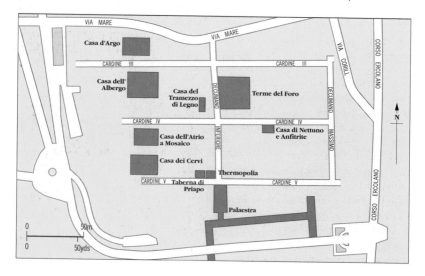

and follow the signs to Scavi di Ercolano. As per the standard rules of Neapolitan driving, finding a parking space will require nerves of steel. If you find somewhere to put your car, park it as soon as you can, even if it means running over one of the numerous black-clad grannies that populate the district. Buses are also available via ANM lines (*www.anm.it*), bus 157 from Piazza Municipio or 255 from Piazza Carlo III. Your best bet is the Circumvesuviana railway from Stazione Circumvesuviana on Corso Garibaldi. If you aren't going on to Pompeii, purchase a Fascia 2 (Zone 2) day pass for €3.10 and get off at Ercolano. This will be valid for your transport to and from the archaeological site and for travel within the city of Naples.

While there is a tourist office in Ercolano, it isn't one of the better ones. Staff at this office will give basic information about the area as well as maps to neighbouring Portici. English usage amongst staff members is limited.

Ercolano itself is best avoided. The town is one of the region's poorest, and architectural interest in the modern high-rises is extremely limited. The main street was at one time an extremely salubrious address for the wealthy of Naples. Considered the heart of the *Miglio d'Oro* (Golden Mile) of residential homes for court members of the Kingdom of the Two Sicilies in the 19th century, Ercolano boasted a bevy of luxurious homes designed by the finest architects of the day. Following the declaration of the Kingdom of Italy in 1860, this stretch of land lost its importance and therefore its residents.

Many of the palaces were abandoned for generations and left to ruin. Today, the avenue and its collection of villas have been left to rot, concealed as they are behind rusting gates and crumbling masonry. Many have been divided up into tiny flats, with little remaining of their original architectural interest.

Herculaneum (Scavi di Ercolano)
Corso Resina 6. Tel: (081) 739 0963. Open: Apr–Oct daily 8.30am–7.30pm; ticket office closes 6pm. Nov–Mar daily 8.30am–5pm; ticket office closes 3.30pm. Admission charge.

House of the Relief of Telephus

Palaestra

HERCULANEUM: A BRIEF HISTORY

Legend has it that the town of Herculaneum was founded by Hercules upon his return from Iberia. Records written by historian Sisenna describe the city as 'built on a small promontory by the sea and bounded by two rivers'. Herculaneum passed through the hands of the conquering Greek and Samnite empires before forming an allegiance with Rome at the end of the Samnite Wars in 290 BC.

Even though only a small section of the town has been excavated, what has been dug up reveals that Herculaneum was a centre of importance to the Roman Empire. Luxurious residences stood on the promontory and there is no evidence of wheel ruts on any of the paved streets to indicate frequent trade or passage of carts. As such, it is believed that Herculaneum was a wealthy residential location for the ultra-rich, chosen for its beauty, tranquillity and healthy environment.

THE BEST SITES
House of the Mosaic Atrium

Named after its beautiful black and white chequerboard mosaic flooring in the atrium, this house is divided into three areas separated by two rows of pillars. In its day, the house enjoyed some of the best views in Herculaneum.

Terme del Foro

Herculaneum's public baths are notable for their stunning mosaics. Of particular note is the Mosaic of Triton in the women's baths.

Casa dei Cervi

Named after its two marble groupings of deer being attacked by hunting dogs, the *Casa dei Cervi* (House of the Deer) is one of the most luxurious residences discovered in Herculaneum. Look for the grand dining room, decorated with frescoes and floored with one of the most elegant pavements in the Roman Empire. Almost all types of marble used during the 1st century AD can be found somewhere in the intricate flooring.

Palaestra

Known more for what it doesn't have than what it does, most of the Palaestra's grandest treasures have been removed and transported to the Museo Nazionale Archeologico for storage. Only partially excavated, the Palaestra has a frontage of 78m (260ft), making it one of the largest buildings in Herculaneum.

Casa del Tramezzo di Legno

Two atria in this house suggest that this building was originally divided into two residences and joined together sometime in the 1st century AD. A wooden partition (now carbonised) can be seen dividing the atrium to create a reception room where the master of the house would conduct his business.

PORTICI

Europe's most densely populated town was devastated in the eruption of Vesuvius in 1631. Luckily a golden age of reconstruction and regal splendour wasn't too far behind. Following the dawn of the Bourbon age, King Charles III ordered a new palace to be built over the wasteland that covered the area. Court life brought the Neapolitan nobility to Portici and a new resort catering to the rich and favoured was born.

No longer the playground paradise it once was, concrete and construction plagues this town, which is literally bursting at its seams. For an idea of what Portici would have looked like, you should head directly to the palace and its grounds; however, you will have

House of Skeletons

UNLOCKING HERCULANEUM

Wear and tear over the years has taken its toll on the ruins of Herculaneum. That fact, combined with the limited funds given to the site by the Italian state, means that only a few of the houses are open on any given day. Much of the town is permanently covered by nasty red fencing, thus ensuring that a number of your photos will be permanently scarred by manufactured reminders of the modern age. A list of buildings is always listed in the ticket office on the Corso Regina. Don't let the list stop you from seeing what you want to see. A small financial gratuity placed surreptitiously in the hands of any of the numerous guards that populate the site should ensure entrance into some of the other locations.

to use a lot of imagination to picture the scene.

Portici was also the home to Italy's first railway line, built in 1839. The original terminus building now houses an excellent railway museum that is enjoyable even for those who aren't fans of transport history.

Museo Ferroviario di Pietarsa

Europe's biggest and best railway museum is housed in the converted terminus building of the first railway line located on the Italian peninsula. Inaugurated in 1839, the 7.4km (4.5 mile) track stretched between Portici and Naples, with factories and workshops installed just over a year later. The museum, built in 1989 to commemorate 150 years of Italian train travel, currently occupies what were the original workshop buildings. All of the buildings have been authentically restored to accommodate the numerous period locomotives on display. Best of the lot are the steam engines, including a painstakingly restored example of the royal train used on the inaugural run in 1839.

For examples of stock from the 20th century, walk across the Mediterranean garden in the central courtyard to Pavilion C.

Via Pietarsa. Tel: (081) 472 003. www.microsys.it/pietrarsa/english/ storia.asp. Open: phone to check dates.

Reggia di Portici and Orto Botanico

The palace that made Portici the heart of the Campanian court no longer sees as much action as it used to. Three architects are known to have worked on this grand villa (Antonio Medrano, Ferdinando Fuga and Luigi Vanvitelli); however, hundreds of other specialists and masons were integral to the splendour that cover the immense façade.

Stretching from the slopes of Vesuvius down to the sea, the grounds boast over 500 species of plants, both native and exotic. The structure originally had two separate sections – designed to take advantage of the stunning views. The lower section faces the sea, while the upper section looks towards Vesuvius. The Reggia was essentially Naples' first archaeological museum, following the discovery of the ruins of Herculaneum, Pompeii and Stabiae. All of the pieces excavated at the various sites during the early years of archaeology in the area were shipped directly to the palace for the pleasure of Charles, his son Ferdinand and the members of the royal court. Since 1873, the palace has been owned by the Faculty of Agriculture of Naples University. To enter the villa, pose as a student or visiting professor and you shouldn't experience too many problems.

Via Università 100. Tel: (081) 775 5135/4850. www.agraria.unina.it. Open: Reggia Sept–July Mon–Fri 8.30am–7pm. Orto Mon–Fri 9am–12.30pm.

Stabiae

When the main coast road was completed, it bypassed the historic town of Castellammare di Stabia and sparked a 30-year decline that the area is still trying to dig itself out of. Once known for its shipyards and spas, the Castellammare is now banking on its proximity to the ancient ruins of Stabiae to ensure its survival. Ferry and hydrofoil services make it a convenient jumping-off point to the islands if you want to avoid the chaos of Naples' Molo Beverello. To get to the Castellammare di Stabia, take the Circumvesuviana train running between Naples and Sorrento. Travel time from Naples is approximately one hour.

The National Railway Museum

Funivia and Monte Faito

The perfect summer getaway for those days when the thermometer soars, Monte Faito is a pleasantly cool set of woodlands set on the higher grounds that overlook town. Enjoy the numerous tree-lined walks and bask in the fresh, alpine air that makes for a nice change from the exhaust-choked fumes that blanket the Campanian coast. Birdwatchers will love the ample opportunities to see robins, nuthatches and other native species that flock here during the summer months. The cable-car ride on the *funivia* is almost enough to warrant the trip alone. Before embarking on any hikes of the peak, make sure to pack enough water and food for the journey, since there are no dining facilities among the many beech-lined paths.

Stazione Circumvesuviana,
Castellammare di Stabia.
Tel: (081) 879 3097. www.vesuviana.it.
Open: daily Apr–mid-June, Sept, Oct
9.25am–4.25pm; mid-June–Aug
7.25am–7.15pm. Closed Nov–Mar.
Admission charge.

Stabiae (Scavi di Castellammare)

Of the digs along the base of Vesuvius, the excavation at Stabiae ranks as one of the most untouched and neglected. Work on Stabiae began at approximately the same time as the discoveries of Pompeii and Herculaneum were made; however, money and skilled workers were taken away from the area during the 18th century in favour of what was believed to be the more significant finds at Pompeii. Excavations resumed in the 1950s, only to be set back yet again

The Reggia

following the earthquakes in 1980. Visitors are limited to only two of the excavated villas, Arianna and San Marco. Most of the grandest artefacts, including frescoes and mosaics, were removed from the villas 200 years ago during the Bourbon reign.

Décor and artwork in Villa San Marco is more impressive than in the walls of neighbouring Arianna; however, there are still great examples to study residential life of times past in both locales. Both villas cover large grounds, as their original owners continually upgraded and added to the existing structures in order to show off their increasing wealth. For a taste of just how opulent the villas were, take a look 50m down along the seaward side for a peek at the nasty housing developments concocted in the 1960s. You will find that the Roman residences compare extremely favourably.

Via Passeggiata Archeologica.
Tel: (081) 871 4541. Open: Apr–Oct daily
8.30am–7.30pm; ticket office closes 6pm.
Nov–Mar daily 8.30am–5pm; ticket office
closes 3.30pm.

Hiking Vesuvius

While the lush green mountainsides of Vesuvius look calm, you shouldn't be fooled. This deceptively innocuous peak has been the cause of the death of thousands, the destruction of numerous homes, and has been the bane of more than just a few empires.

Vesuvius could erupt at any time, according to the experts at the Osseratorio Vesuviano, the institute that has monitored the volcano's activity since 1841. And even though locals have slowly reclaimed Vesuvius' slopes, you shouldn't follow in their footsteps: while 700,000 residents call the slopes of Vesuvius home, you can be pretty sure that the population figure will fall if and when Vesuvius decides to erupt again. When Vesuvius does decide to wake up, experts believe that ash and lava won't constitute the greatest risk. Rather, it will be a rapidly moving, super-heated cloud of gases that will cause the most destruction – much like the one in AD 79.

No visible reminders of the volcano's hazards have remained since the last time Vesuvius decided to blow her top in 1944. There is no plume of smoke, flowing lava or floating ash; even the vegetation has grown back, with native plants returning to the rich volcanic soil located at the top of the cone.

A walk up the peak is a popular pastime and well worth considering even if you aren't a regular hiker. Declared a UNESCO Biosphere Reserve, the volcano is a protected plot of land attracting 200,000 visitors each year. Hiking is permitted right up to the rim of the

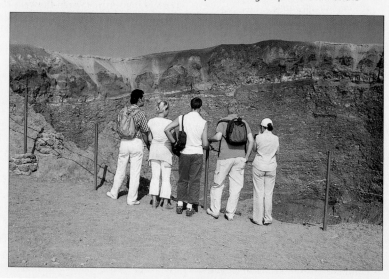

services up Vesuvius from Piazza Anfiteatro in Pompeii, passing by the Ercolano station on the Circumvesuviana train line. From this route you can visit both the Observatory and get dropped off at the car park to begin your hike. One-way transport from Pompeii costs €3: from Ercolano the cost is €1.70. By car, drive along the A3 motorway to Ercolano and follow the signs to Parco Nazionale del Vesuvio.

Cratere del Vesuvio

Tel: (081) 777 5720. Open: daily 9am–2hrs before sunset. Admission charge. Note that trips to the crater are suspended during bad weather.

Museo dell'Osservatorio Vesuviano

Tel: (081) 777 7149. www.ov.ingv.it. Open: Sat, Sun 10am–1pm.

cone, allowing visitors to peak down into the depths of the crater 200m (700ft) below. Best in May and early June, Vesuvius should be tackled in the early morning on calm, clear days. Windy days are not advised, as conditions on the exposed rim during these periods can be critical. The standard 30-minute route runs between the 'Quota 1,000' car park and the rim along a well-maintained, curving path. The car park is located at the end of the road on the mountain's western side. An interesting museum and observatory, chronicling eruptions of times past and the history of volcanic study, is located on the way to the car park along the western road. The Bourbon-period building in which it is located has survived at least seven eruptions and countless generations of smoke, fire and lava.

Bus and car are the best ways of getting to the area. Transporti Vesuviani (*Tel: (081) 559 2582*) runs regular

Opposite and above: Hiking up Vesuvius is a popular pastime
Below: Colourful volcanic rock

Capri

'Capri combines, in a granite basket, all the most colourful and fragrant species of Mediterranean flora. It is a land naturally dedicated to the repose of the mind and the delight of the senses, an *Insula Beatorum*, a floating Garden of Eden.' So wrote Alberto Savinio: popular since Roman times, so much has been written about this craggy corner of Campania.

Ciao bella!

During the Romantic period, writers, artists and poets flocked to the island to experience the 'lost sensuality' portrayed by the topography and Capri's inhabitants. Capri's modern-day popularity was cemented in the 19th century with the discovery of the *Grotta Azzura* (Blue Grotto), but its sun-drenched shores had been beckoning tourists and travellers for at least two millennia before that time.

From remotely Roman to courtly capital

Capri captivated a number of Roman emperors, but none more so than Tiberius, who spent the last ten years of his life ruling the empire from his Villa Jovis. Tiberius ruled by using a courier service and was unseen by citizens of the capital, fuelling rumours of his scandalous lifestyle – rumours that weren't entirely unfounded. Following his death, the island fell into a long period of decline. From the Middle Ages onwards, the rocky shores fell into the hands of a number of rulers and were the scene of more than just a few skirmishes, most notably between the English and the French during the Napoleonic wars.

Invasion of the tourist

Capri was far from ready to deal with the mass tourist influx that coincided with its popularity in the romantic literature of the 19th century. As writers such as Henry James and Goethe spread the word about Capri's trappings and charms, tourists travelled to the sleepy island to find out what all the fuss was about – and they haven't left since. The invention of the hydrofoil was the best (or worst, depending on how you see it) boost for local tourism, as the months between June and September see up to 50,000 visitors descend upon the land mass every day. Every year the mayor of Capri announces plans to limit daily visitor levels to a more manageable level: and every year absolutely nothing is done. No matter how many people decide to hit Capri, the rocky topography and small-scale agriculture translates into a number of quiet nooks and crannies available for exploration.

Luxurious lifestyles

In order to maintain its exclusive reputation, the hotels of Capri charge notoriously outrageous prices: a simple coffee on the *piazzetta* can cost an arm and a leg in high season. Traditionally, those who want to 'see and be seen' stick to the properties around Capri, while fans of solitude and a more down-to-earth atmosphere head over to the

agricultural trappings of Anacapri. But the big draw of the island continues to be the fabled Blue Grotto, 'discovered' by a Polish poet called Klopisch, but known by the residents and fishermen of the island for years. A typical visit to the Blue Grotto takes about two hours out of your sun-bathing and shopping time, with numerous boats departing from the Marina Grande throughout the day.

Arco Naturale

The Basics of Capri

There are a number of ways to get to the island of Capri. The most common method is via the numerous ferries and hydrofoils that ply the waves between the major ports of Campania and Capri's Marina Grande. From Naples' main commuter port, the Molo Beverello, departures run throughout the day. There is also a scheduled service from Mergellina and the western end of the bay.

View from Monte Solaro

Should Naples prove incompatible with your itinerary, you can reach the 'playground of the rich' from Sorrento, Ischia and the Amalfi Coast ports of Salerno, Amalfi and Positano. For daily updated timetables, check the Naples newspaper *Il Mattino*. Once on the island, the Capri tourist board provides a wealth of information, including a listing of all return sea schedules. Before you arrive in Naples, check out the Capri tourist board website (*www.capritourism.com*) for seasonal crossing times and prices. While services from Naples run all year, transport between the Amalfi Coast, Ischia and Capri only runs in high season, from April to October.

Schedules and services

From the Amalfi Coast: LMS (*Tel: Amalfi (089) 873 301/ Salerno (089) 234 892/(089) 227 979*) run hydrofoils between Amalfi, Positano, Salerno and Capri. Consorzio Linee Marittime (*Tel: (089) 873 301*) runs hydrofoils from Positano only. Journeys take approximately 30 minutes.

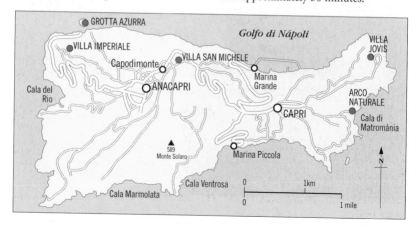

Punta Carena

Family fun at Marina Piccola

From Ischia: Alilauro (*Tel: (081) 991 888*) runs one hydrofoil and two ferries a day from Ischia Porto. Hydrofoils take 40 minutes to make the crossing, while ferries take 90 minutes.

From Naples: Caremar (*Tel: (081) 551 3882*), NLG Linea Jet (*Tel: (081) 552 7209*) and SPAV (*Tel: (081) 761 2348*) are the main companies that run between the Molo Beverello and Capri. In summer, hydrofoils run hourly between the Molo's central quay and the Marina Grande. SPAV also runs hydrofoils from Mergellina every two hours in high season. By hydrofoil, the crossing time is approximately 40 minutes.

If you prefer using a ferry, Caremar is the company to choose. Six daily ferries run all year round from Beverello – three of which are high-speed *traghetti veloci* (50 minutes); the others take 1 hour 20 minutes. Ferries are both cheaper and the only option in rough weather. Last boats from Naples usually leave at 8.30pm in winter and 9.30pm in summer.

From Sorrento: Caremar (*Tel: (081) 807 3077*) and LMP Alilauro (*Tel: (081) 878 1430/(081) 807 3024*) make the 20-minute crossing from Sorrento's Marina Piccola to Capri. In summer, hydrofoils leave on an hourly basis.

By helicopter: The transport option of choice for visiting dignitaries, Hollywood celebrities and Middle Eastern royalty is also the most

expensive. The cost of a one-way flight accommodating up to four people from Capodichino airport to the Anacapri heliport is €862.
Contact Cab air, tel: (081) 584 4355/ www.cabair.it

By water taxi: If you're in a rush or travelling out of season, water taxis are available from most ports on the Campanian coast. Taxi del Mare (*Tel: (081) 877 3600/www.taxidelmare.it*) is the most common line, offering a fleet of ten-seat speedboats at a rate of €26 per nautical mile. A typical run from Sorrento to Capri will set you back about €208 one way.

Getting around

Capri town is closed to all forms of motorised transport beyond the bus terminus on Via Roma. One exception to this rule (and a great help to people with various mobility problems) is the electric trolleys that transport luggage between the marina and the numerous hotels.

Five-star properties usually offer porters at quayside, should you require them. If you have a large amount of luggage, you should take advantage of this service, as the cliffs of Capri are quite steep and difficult to traverse, especially during the tourist-choked peak season when waiting times to use

The Piazzetta

the funicular railway can get long. Look for the name of your hotel on the cap of the porters as you disembark from your ferry or hydrofoil. Anacapri hotels offer minibuses to bring you and your luggage directly to the door. Otherwise, the funicular, buses and taxis are all available at the end of the quay. If you are planning to do a lot of touring around the island, take advantage of the Unico Capri public transport ticket, available from the funicular ticket office. Tickets come in three options – single trip, 60 minutes and day-pass – and can be used throughout the entire network.

Circle-island boat tours: Circuit tours of the island can be booked at the Marina Grande from a number of tour operators. Tours sometimes include the Blue Grotto, depending upon weather conditions. Prices start at €9 per person.

By bus: There are six bus routes that can take you to most corners of Capri. The three main services that run most frequently are Marina Grande-Capri (*7am–midnight*), Marina Grande-Anacapri (*7am–8pm*) and Capri-Anacapri (*6.30am–midnight*). The other three routes of Capri-Marina Piccola, Anacapri-Grotta Azzura (Blue Grotto) and Anacapri-Punta Carena run less frequently, especially in the off season. For information call SIPPIC (*Tel: (081) 837 0420*), except for the Blue Grotto and Punta Carena lines, which are operated by Staiano (*Tel: (081) 837 1544*).

By funicular railway: From the main Marina Grande station, funiculars tackle the climb to Capri town every 15 minutes (*Oct–Mar 6.30am–9pm; Apr, May 6.30am–9.30pm; June–Sept 6.30am–12.30am*). The funicular is

The ferry to Capri

operated by SIPPIC. *For information, tel: (081) 837 0420.*

By scooter: If you have the guts to try it out, a scooter can be the fastest and most economical way of getting around Capri. Rent a scooter at Rent an Electric Scooter (*Via Roma 68. Tel: (081) 837 5863*). Scooter rentals cost €8 per hour, including a helmet. A driving licence is not required. As the scooters are electric, they have a limited range of 50km (31 miles) before they need recharging at the base: but don't worry about getting

stranded, as this is a lot of distance on this tiny land mass.

By taxi: Capri's taxi fleet is one of the best-looking in the business. Open-topped vehicles can take you anywhere on the island – albeit at a price. The tiny streets make overtaking almost impossible, so if you get stuck behind a slow-moving vehicle, be prepared for a long journey and a high fare. Typical rates are €15 from the port to Capri town or Anacapri, and €100 for a circle-island tour.

Capri is a big tourist draw

THE *GROTTA AZZURA* (BLUE GROTTO)

Capri legend has it that Polish poet August Kopisch and Swiss artist Ernest Fries discovered the Blue Grotto in 1826 after swimming here accompanied by a local hotel owner and fisherman. Truth be told, islanders had known about Capri's most famous sight for centuries – a landing stage and small, rough-hewn nymphaeum dating back to the period of the Roman Empire can be found at the back of the Grotto – and often played practical jokes on visitors exploring the area. Local writer Raffaele la Capria backs this claim, suggesting

that the discovery of the grotto was merely a prank played on the two artists after being lured by tales of 'a cave inhabited by the devil… and by strange marine creatures'.

Today, a ride to the Blue Grotto requires more than just an eager guide. The most common method of reaching the cave is by motor launch from the Marina Grande. The three-stage journey involves a quick motorboat ride to the Grotto, a transfer to a four-seater rowboat and a lightning-flash row under the low-lying cave entrance into the mystical blue beyond. The whole trip costs about €14. You can save yourself

Boats at the Blue Grotto

€1.50 by taking the bus from the Marina Grande, changing at Anacapri for travel to the car park above the Grotto. While you may not save much money, it makes for a delightful way to familiarize yourself with the lay of the island. Tours of the Blue Grotto, including travel time to and from the famed cave, take about an hour and a half. For maximum time inside the cave, avoid the peak season and/or plan your visit late in the day or during the lunch hour when demand to get inside the grotto is at its lowest.

The grotto owes its exalted position in Capri's list of tourism draws primarily to the wealth of literature and writing dedicated to its enchanted qualities. One anonymous 19th-century English traveller outlined the best way of seeing the grotto's delights by stating that 'a visit requires a cloudless day, a resplendent sea in a placid bay, the dazzling skies of Italy should abate, and the very breezes be calm and still'. The anonymous traveller got it quite right when describing ideal conditions as the mystical blue appearance of the grotto is caused by the refraction of light. Calm seas translate into greater refraction and a more intense blue colour on the walls of the grotto and vault.

Theoretically, you can still enjoy a visit into the grotto by swimming through the entrance after paying the standard €4 entrance fee. Kopisch and Fries may have enjoyed this method of examining the grotto's trappings back in 1826, but today's intrepid few are advised not to attempt this foolhardy way of entering the cave. Strong currents and the possibility that the boatmen

The famous cave

who transport tourists in their sturdy rowboats may clop you on the head with one of their oars are the two biggest reasons to prevent you from donning your bathing costume.

High winds and rough seas close the grotto on a regular basis, especially between November and March. Check postings at the Marina Grande for further details.

Grotta Azzura (Blue Grotto)
Open: daily 9am–1hr before sunset.
Admission charge.

Capri may be the playground of today's nouveau riche, but the level of excess seen in modern-day hotels, yachts and restaurants pales in comparison to the hedonism of yesteryear. The island's salacious history dates back to AD 27, when Emperor Tiberius visited Capri during a tour of southern Italy. Tiberius was so enchanted by Capri's people and geography that he moved himself and his entire court to the island to live out the last ten years of his life here.

During his time on Capri, Tiberius developed a number of strange and highly erotic tastes, often demanding large groups of young male and female servants 'perform' in front of him. When that failed to appease his voyeuristic nature, he wandered through the grounds of his lush villa complex – the Villa Jovis – to enjoy the numerous erotic statues, Egyptian love manuals and descriptive paintings.

Love hurts

After earthly pleasures, torture was second on Tiberius' list of favourite things to do. Torture rooms, prisons and execution chambers existed in all of the villas owned by Tiberius on the island. The 330m (1,155ft) Salto di Tiberio precipice, found at the end of a long loggia in the northern end of the Villa Jovis grounds, is thought to have been where enemies of the state were thrown to their death into the rock-strewn waters below.

Pink Capri

While loved by the effete American author Truman Capote, Capri is no longer the pink Mecca it once was. The mid-20th-century decades saw the straight literary set move in, banishing the gay community to other more accepting locales. In their place arrived Maxim Gorky, Lenin and a collection of Russian émigrés, author Graham Greene and Curzio Malaparte – an Italian Ernest Hemingway, famous for his exploits in the 1940s and 50s.

THE KRUPP AFFAIR

Greeks and Sapphics weren't the only ones to bring scandal to the shores of Capri. Friedrich Alfred Krupp (1854–1902), a German steel heir and industrialist, was so intoxicated by the island that he built a roadway from the steps of his private villa down to the Mediterranean. Hewn from the rocky slopes of the island, the Via Krupp winds its way down from the heights of Capri to the Marina Piccola. The breathtaking, yet narrow, road remains one of Capri's most pleasant walks – unfortunately, Krupp's personal fate wasn't as 'happily ever after'. In 1902, Krupp committed suicide after accusations were raised that he had been taking part in orgies in one of the island's grottoes. It is still unknown to this day as to whether Krupp was involved in the scandal or if the accusations were part of a political plot to smear his name.

Opposite top: The view from Villa Jovis
Opposite bottom and above: The beautiful people still flock to Capri
Below: The home of Curzio Malaparte

CAPRI TOWN

Capri Town is both the height of
luxury and an example of how awful
the tourism industry can get. Packed
with five-star celebrities and no-star
package-trippers, the place still manages
to draw in a who's who eager to figure
out what's what.

Marina Grande

Almost everyone's first port of call upon
reaching Capri is the bustling Marina
Grande. During the high season, the
marina is a hellish mass of humanity.
Get out as fast as you can – and that
might take a while, judging by the usual

Casa Rosa

length of queues to get on the funicular
up to the centre of town. If you are
looking to tour around the island, then
you're in the right place. From the
Marina Grande, you can purchase boat
tours, hire a taxi, catch a bus to
Anacapri or purchase public transit
passes from the main ticket office.

Piazzetta

Look to the left as you emerge from the
funicular station at the far end of the Via
Roma. Here you will find Capri's 'see
and be seen' heart, the Piazzetta. Packed
with cafés and pedestrians, the Piazzetta
is the archetypal Mediterranean town
square. Four rival bars, indistinguishable
from each other except by their
different-coloured chairs, take over the
square, providing the best opportunities
for gossip and catching up on the latest
in couture fashion trends. While the
coffees are expensive, the social theatre
on display will more than make up for
the exorbitant cost.

Capri's parish church, Santo Stefano
(*open: daily 8am–8pm*) is located on
the south side of the Piazzetta. There
isn't much of note about the Baroque
architecture, other than the fact that
it was built on the same site as an
earlier church.

Via Vittorio Emmanuele III

Capri's main street runs south from the
Piazzetta past dozens of high-fashion
boutiques and *limoncello* souvenir
outlets. Some of the big names to look
out for include Cavalli, Dolce &
Gabbana, Zegna and Gucci. Most of the
clothing boutiques are stocked with the
dregs of the collections – suitable only if

The view from Scala Fenicia

your Vuitton luggage was accidentally lost in the first-class check-in lounge.

Certosa di San Giacomo

This ancient monastery at the eastern end of the Via Matteotti was built by a monastic order that was established in 1371 by Count Giacomo Arcucci, the powerful secretary to Queen Joan I. Islanders have never held strong affections for the residents of the monastery, often coming into conflict with them over the island's hunting and grazing rights.

During the plague of 1656, tensions reached a high point as the monks locked their doors to the outside world, refusing to tend to Capri's sick and dying in the hope of saving their own lives. In response, locals threw the bodies of the plague-infested dead over the monastery walls.

Villa Jovis

An easy walk from Capri town is the Roman home of Emperor Tiberius, the Villa Jovis. From the Piazzetta, the Via Botteghe leads past the Chapel of San Michele. Follow the path past the church until the houses thin out and the hike gets steep. The actual villa isn't as impressive as it most certainly once was; however, you can still see the Salto di Tiberio – a precipice from which Tiberius executed criminals – and remnants of huge cisterns that guaranteed the self-sufficiency of the complex.

ANACAPRI

Anacapri retains a distinct small-town feel in comparison to its more upmarket neighbour, thanks to the fact that it was separated from the rest of the island by an impervious wall of cliffs until a connecting road was finally built in 1877. Less village and more a collection of small-scale farmers and residents, Anacapri is the laid-back vacation alternative on the island. Mentioning the word *dolce* here will bring you a luscious pastry, and not a luscious designer gown from the catwalks of Milan.

Rural residents and Caprese rivals

The *anacapresi* are fiercely independent individuals. For years, locals preferred to travel to the Neapolitan ports in search of work rather than owe their salaries to the enemy *caprese* a few miles down the island. Until the construction of the inter-island road, the only means of getting to the remote cliff-side community was via the Scala Fenicia, a steep set of stairs that leads up from the Marina Grande. Travellers from Anacapri to Naples were forced to go through the port, deep in enemy territory, whenever they needed to visit the mainland.

Fame and fortune

Anacapri owes its illustrious reputation to the writings of the 19th-century Swedish doctor Axel Munthe. While researching his book *The Story of San Michele*, he encountered the local postmistress on the street. She informed him that she had 'once been down to Capri – but it hadn't impressed her much'. Munthe later incorporated this

A corner of the Villa San Michele gardens

episode into his work and translated his tales of life in the southern climes into over 30 different languages. The book is littered with representations of the quirky rural folk that inhabited this tiny corner of the island back in the 19th century. Northern Europeans in turn flocked to the tiny village to discover its rural charms.

San Michele Arcangelo

The town's major church is a piece of Baroque splendour, boasting a wonderful majolica mosaic floor based around the theme of earthly Paradise. Built in 1761, the floor is a particular favourite with children, due to the numerous representations of exotic animals in the brightly coloured tiles. *Piazza San Nicola. Tel: (081) 837 2396. Open: daily July–Oct 10am–7pm; Nov–Mar 9.30am–4pm; Apr–June 9.30am–5pm. Admission charge.*

Villa San Michele

Making his fortune as the hottest society doctor in Paris, Munthe moved to Anacapri 15 years after first setting foot in the village in 1874. Using the funds he had built up in his prime medical practice, he built the Villa San Michele on the grounds of one of Tiberius' original 12 Capri villas. The architecture mixes Renaissance and Romanesque influences with a large number of statues.

The actual building isn't worth more than a cursory exploration, but the views are definitely worth the trip. The villa and gardens are kept meticulously clean, thanks to a Swedish foundation that keeps the Munthe flame alive. Try to time your visit with the Friday-evening classical music concerts held in the gardens during the summer.

Viale Axel Munthe. Tel: (081) 837 1401. www.sanmichele.org. Open: daily May–Sept 9am–6pm; Apr, Oct 9.30am–5pm; Nov–Feb 10.30am–3.30pm; Mar 9.30am–4pm. Admission charge.

Villa San Michele

Ischia

Lying at the western end of the Bay of Naples, Ischia, along with the neighbouring islands of Procida and Vivara, forms the Phlegraean archipelago. The volcanoes that formed the bays, sheer cliffs and caves are now extinct, yet the geothermal springs remain, drawing thousands of tourists each year to the healing waters.

Ferry to Ischia

While the island of Capri has always had an intoxicating effect on those who visit its shores, Ischia has historically been more of a slow-burning destination. When the Greeks arrived in the 8th century BC, they quickly departed in favour of the mainland camp at Cumae. The island's seismic activity and population of indigenous residents didn't suit the newcomers at all, even though Ischia was ideally suited as a strategic position on the Mediterranean trade routes.

During the Roman era, the island finally found fame through its geothermally heated waters. It retains this reputation today through the huge number of spas and hydrotherapy centres that continue to populate the area.

The last eruptions on the island occurred in 1302. Fearing another Pompeii, residents fled to the mainland in Baia, only returning to the Ischian shores four years later when they gathered on the rock of the Castello Aragonese – a castle built to protect Ischia from the constant invasions of foreign powers and pirates.

Ischia fell into the hands of various conquering foes throughout the

centuries, eventually succumbing to the British allies of King Ferdinand following a decade of French rule. The British took years to oust their hated enemies from the island, bringing intense devastation. Evidence of their bombardment can still be seen on the castle's walls.

The north coast of the island remains the most populated coast, due to the easy access to the sea and picture-perfect views of the Phlegraean Fields on the mainland. The best day to celebrate its climate, thermal waters and stunning beaches is 26 July – the date of the procession to honour Ischia's patron saint, Sant'Anna.

Procida

Covering less than four square kilometres, Procida is the most densely inhabited island in the Med. The sea and its treasures provide the bulk of the island's employment opportunities – the island has produced fishermen and merchant sailors for generations – with luxury yachts pouring into the new Marina Grande on a daily basis.

First populated by the Greeks, small fishing villages prone to attack were

W H AUDEN

Writer W H Auden spent almost all of his time between the years of 1948 and 1957 on Ischia. Renowned as a haven for homosexuals seeking sinful pleasures, Auden arrived on Ischia's rocky shores and fell in love with the sleepy fishing village of Forio, calling it 'one of the loveliest spots on earth'. His love affair with the island fell apart after he hired a notoriously handsome local boy named Giocondo to look after his house. In 1956, Giocondo tried to cash a cheque Auden had given him. Giocondo claimed it was for 'services rendered', causing fury amongst island residents and the parish priest. The feud and disgust caused Auden to flee the island for Austria, never to return. 'I don't like sunshine,' he commented. 'I would like Mediterranean life in a northern climate.'

built on the island's shores. Locals quickly realised that life on the high grounds was the only possible defence against invaders and proceeded to pack up their homes in favour of hillside residences. Despite continuing raids, the island developed a prosperous shipbuilding and fishing industry. Procida continued to experience periodic raids and pirating until the Bourbon age when the royal family purchased the Castello d'Avalos and turned the area into a hunting reserve. Locals were banned from owning cats that might destroy the stock of pheasants and were subjected to heavy fines. Needless to say, the Bourbons weren't exactly well loved by the local populace. By this time, however, the bulk of Procida's residences were owned by prosperous vacationing mainlanders who built summer homes on the island's rocky shores.

Cathedral del'Assunta, Ischia

Torre Michelangelo, on the coast opposite Castello Aragonese

Today, the Good Friday procession is Procida's claim to fame. The *Processione dei Misteri* involves a life-size wooden sculpture of Christ on the cross, carried by local fishermen to the Marina Grande under a black veil. Other wooden sculptures follow the main statue, carried by men dressed in white cloaks with turquoise capes and children in medieval costume.

You won't need any form of transport other than your own two feet on Procida – the island is that small. A complete circuit around the island takes approximately four hours, if you're fit.

A brief word of warning to anyone contemplating a trip during peak season: while Procida is the least visited of all the islands in the region, it is also the smallest. Consequently, the shores are practically heaving with humanity, exploding from a year-round population of 11,000 to almost 20,000 in August. Despite this, there are still undiscovered pockets to explore, even during the height of summer. Enjoy watching the daily catch come in, as you sit at one of the cafés that line the Marina Grande, or savour a stroll through one of the inland lemon groves and you'll be sure to fall in love with Procida's numerous charms.

Procida's Marina Grande

BE YOUR OWN CAPTAIN

If a luxury yacht isn't within your budget or you're short of that million or two to sail your way around the Med, don't fret! Procida may be a tiny island, but it's big on choice when it comes to chartering your own boat. Its new yacht marina – the biggest in Campania – has drawn a number of savvy entrepreneurs to its snazzy docks, making it an excellent locale to arrange an Italian sailing holiday. Rental periods can cover anything from a day-trip to a month-long cruise. Choose your own adventure with the following rental outfits:

Ippocampo

Lato ponente (west side), Marina Chiaiolella. Tel: (081) 810 1437. Email: amedeoippocampo@tisca.linet.it. Open: daily 9am–7pm. Closed mid-Oct–Mar. No credit cards. Rates start at €62 per day.

Sailitalia Procida

Via Roma 10, Marina Grande. Tel: (081) 896 9962. www.sailitalia.com. Open: Mon–Fri 9.30am–1pm, 3–7 pm. No credit cards. Rates from €992 per week.

The Basics of Ischia

Ischia is as easy to get to as Capri – the only difference being in the companies that choose to ply the waters between the mainland and Ischia Porto and/or Casamicciola. Departures to and from Capri, Sorrento and Procida are also available, albeit far less frequently.

Castello Aragonese

During low season inter-island departures may be terminated, so it is best to check in advance if you are planning a complicated itinerary. From the main commuter port of Naples, the Molo Beverello, departures run throughout the day. There is also a scheduled service from Pozzuoli and the western end of the bay. For daily updated timetables, check the Naples newspaper *Il Mattino*.

Schedules and services
From Naples, Pozzuoli, Capri, Sorrento and Procida: Caremar (*Tel: (081) 551 3882; www.gruppotirrenia.it/caremar/html/home/mainframeset.htm*), Lauro (*Tel: (081) 551 3352; www.lauro.it*) and Traghetti Pozzuoli (*Tel: (081) 526 7736*) are the main companies that run hydrofoil and car ferry services between the mainland, the Bay of Naples archipelago and the Ischian ports of Porto and Casamicciola. Hydrofoils run hourly between the Molo's central quay and Ischia Porto. By hydrofoil, the crossing time is approximately 45 minutes. The cost of a crossing is approximately €11, depending on the company.

If you are planning on transporting your car, ferries are your only option, and they take approximately 1hr 35min to complete the journey. Ferries are also cheaper, and they are the only option in rough weather. Tickets start at €7 if you are travelling without a car. Last boats from Naples usually leave at 8.30pm in winter and 9.30pm in summer. A charge applies if you make an advance booking – well worth it during high season weekends. Note that none of the companies accepts credit cards.

By water taxi: If you're in a rush or travelling out of season and are pressed for time, water taxis are available from most ports on the Campanian coast. Taxi del Mare (*Tel: (081) 877 3600; www.taxidelmare.it*) offers a fleet of ten-seater speedboats at a rate of €26 per nautical mile.

Circle-island boat tours: If you would like to see Ischia from a different perspective, consider a boat trip around the island with Sogema (*Tel: (081) 985 80; www.ischiasogema.it*). Tickets cost €12 for a circle-Ischia tour, or €21 for a day-trip to Capri.

Getting around by bus: Ischia's public transport services are run by Sepsa (*Tel: (081) 991 828*). The two main routes you are likely to encounter are the Circolare sinistra, which circles the island in an anticlockwise direction from Ischia Porto, and the Circolare destra, which does the same route clockwise. Stops include Casamicciola, Lacco Ameno, Forio, Serrara, Fontana and Barano.

Services run every 30 minutes (every 15 during the rush hour) and tend to get packed during the high season. Other services include routes from Ischia Porto to Sant'Angelo (every

15 minutes), Giardini Poseidon to Citara (every 30 minutes) and spiaggia dei Maronti via Testaccio (every 20 minutes).

Minibus services run within Ischia Porto, Ponte and Forio. Tickets are required before boarding and can be purchased at the terminus in Ischia Porto, at tabacchi stores and in newsstands. At time of writing, tickets cost €0.93 (single-trip), €1.65 (half-day), €2.74 (24hr), €11.88 (weekly pass) and €16.53 (two-week pass).

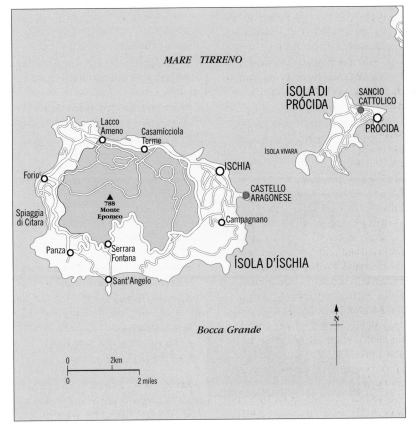

If you're looking for the ultimate in relaxation, then you've come to the right place. Ischia has been famous for its thermal baths since the days of the Roman Empire, when visitors would flock to the bubbling pools that dot the island for healing and curative rest. Thanks to the geothermal power of the Phlegraean Fields, Ischia (then called Aenaria) was the area's most popular holiday resort for the rich and unwell. Its mysteriously soothing powers remain popular today – even if hedonists come just for the pleasure of a soak in a naturally warm hot tub.

True connoisseurs have a favourite rest stop, selecting their top-bath list according to mineral content and success rates in curing particular ailments. But, with 103 hot springs available on the island, you'll have plenty of options to choose from. Unfortunately for people on a tight budget, most of the hot springs have been commandeered by hotels and resorts that allow access only to paying guests, but there are still a few open to all if you look for them. The following are some of the better possibilities:

Negombo
Via Baia di San Montano, Lacco Ameno. Tel: (081) 986 152; www.negombo.it. Open: daily 8.30am–7pm. Closed mid-Oct–mid-Apr. Admission charge.
A public spa open to day visitors. Entrance allows access to a stunning garden filled with hundreds of exotic plants, the San Montano beach and the obligatory thermal spa facilities.

Parco Termale Aphrodite Apollon
Via Petrelle, Sant'Angelo. Tel: (081) 999 219; www.aphrodite.it. Open: daily Apr–Oct 8.30am–6pm. Admission charge.
A popular option for fans of letting it all hang out, the Parco Termale offers a nude bathing area, massages and medical treatment. Free boat-taxis from Sant'Angelo are included in the admission fee. Saunas, a gymnasium and 12 pools are available with the purchase of a day pass.

Terme Belliazzi
Piazza Bagni 134, Casamicciola. Tel: (081) 994 580. Open: May–Oct Mon–Sat 7am–noon, 5–6.30pm. Closed Nov–Apr. Admission charge.

If you want to experience what drew Roman tourists, then visit the baths of the Terme Belliazzi. Built over the site of the original ancient Roman pools, the architecture is firmly neoclassical in tone, looking much like a temple in honour of the body. Massages, whirlpools and mud treatments are all on offer to those who want a little extra.

Terme della Regina Isabella

Piazza San Restituta, Lacco Ameno.
Tel: (081) 994 322; www.reginaisabella.it
Open: Mon–Sat 8am–12.15pm,
5–7.30pm; Sun 8am–12.15pm.
Closed Nov–Mar. Admission charge.
A rare example of a hotel that allows entrance to day visitors who purchase a pass. All of the usual treatments and baths are on offer, albeit in a slightly grander style than you might normally get in some of the other public-access properties. Prices of a day pass are slightly higher than in other locations, but in this instance you most certainly get what you pay for.

Terme di Cava Scura

Via Cava Scura, Spiaggia dei Maronti,
Serrara Fontana. Tel: (081) 905 564.
Open: mid-Apr–Oct daily
8.30am–1.30pm, 2.30–6pm. Closed
Nov–mid-Apr. Admission charge.
Ischia's most naturally beautiful spa, the Terme di Cava Scura is hewn out of rugged cliffs located at the end of one of Ischia's most stunning hikes. Designed for the truly knowledgeable spa-goer, treatments on offer include massages, facials and thermal baths in divine locations – including a natural cave.

Opposite: The cove at Negombo
Above: Termale Aphrodite

North Ischia

Always the busiest part of the island, the north coast of Ischia boasts a number of sights and villages to explore, suitable both for day-trippers and those on an extended stay. Once two separate towns (Villa dei Bagni and Borgo Celsi), the main strip of hotels and shops has been combined into one administrative centre known as Ischia Porto and Ponte. This area incorporates the entire stretch of coast between the ferry port and the Castello Aragonese.

Castello Aragonese

Originally fortified by the Greeks in the 5th century BC, this rocky outcrop has been used as a stronghold by just about every group, empire or army intent on conquering the area. Romans, Goths and Arabs have all had their hands on the Castello – but never for very long.

The Castello found fame in the 16th century when it became home to the court of Vittoria Colonna, the wife of Ischia's feudal lord, Ferrante d'Avalos. Vittoria had a strong – albeit platonic – relationship with Michelangelo, who ensured her memory would live on in his work. 'Nature, that never made so fair a face, remained ashamed, and tears were in all eyes,' he wrote after watching Vittoria pass away in 1574.

With the Saracens a constant threat to Ischia's fragile population, the Castello became a refuge of sorts, calling itself home to 2,000 families. Even after the Saracen menace disappeared in the 18th century, locals insisted on staying within its formidable walls.

It took 100 years for the families to move out, leaving behind about 13 churches and a few nuns to run the place. The British managed to damage the Castello more than any other invading force during their bombardment of the island in 1809. Determined to rid Ischia of its French 'rulers', they attacked the Castello: you can still see the scars of their aggressive actions pockmarked on the walls. Following the success of the British military plan, the fortress was transformed

Flora at La Mortella

into a prison to accommodate French prisoners of war.

Tel: (081) 992 834. Open: Mar–Nov daily 9.30am–1hr before sunset; also 10 days over the Christmas season. Admission charge.

The main port

Until 1854, Ischia's main port was an inland lake formed by an extinct volcanic crater. The waters, due to the geothermal activity of the area, were particularly smelly. King Ferdinand II was so repulsed by the odour that he ordered that an opening should be constructed linking the waters to the sea. And so a port was born.

Ischia's main street is the **Via Roma**. Pedestrianised to accommodate the hustle and bustle of activity during the high season, it is lined with numerous exclusive shops and hotels. North of the Via Roma is where you will find the town's main beach. Take any of the lanes leading off the street to find your way there.

If you need a break from the beating sun, follow the traffic to the junction with Via d'Avalos. A gate just off the main strip leads to a lush (and slightly unkempt) garden in the grounds of the **Villa Nenzi Bozzi**, which is filled with shady trees. *The gardens are open daily from 7am–8pm.*

Forio is Ischia's leading wine-production area

Forio and the west

Forio is the largest town on Ischia, with a year-round population of 20,000 people. Twelve ancient watchtowers line the coast near the Ischian 'metropolis', originally built to help guard the city's population against the constant Saracen attacks that plagued the area. The best example that remains standing today is **Il Torrione**, dating from around 1480.

While there are 17 churches to choose from in town, most have been highly remodelled and no longer feature original artwork. The one exception is the church of **Santa Maria del Soccorso**. Originally a 14th-century Augustinian convent, its white outline in the centre of a large viewing platform makes it one of the most romantic churches on the island.

The beach at Poseidon Gardens

The narrow road leading to Monte Epomeo gives some idea of the importance of wine-making in the region – and the length of time residents have lived in the area building the industry up to its current peak. The meandering roadway is lined with vines covering a number of rock-cut troglodyte dwellings, and evidence of habitation goes as far back as the Stone Age. Today, Forio is Ischia's leading wine-producing centre.

Before you leave town, be sure not to miss the **fumaroles of Neptune** and the thermal complex in the **Bay of Citara**. Botanists should also add the gardens of **La Mortella** to their list of 'must-sees'. The lush, green space calls itself home to more than 3,000 types of plant, most of which are extremely rare.

La Mortella
Via F Calise 35, Forio. Tel: (081) 986 220; www.ischia.it/mortella. Open: Apr–mid-Nov Tue, Thur, Sat, Sun 9am–7pm. Concerts: Apr, June, Sept–Oct Sat & Sun 5pm; arrive 30 min prior, to ensure seating. Admission charge.

Monte Epomeo and the southwest
Monte Epomeo is Ischia's highest peak at 787m (2,582ft). Lying to the east of Forio, the mountain can be traversed by taking via Monterone or Via Bocca to the paths that lead through the Falanga forest to the summit. Note, however, that the paths are poorly marked and easy to miss, so keep your eyes peeled.

If you find the town-centre beaches a little too crowded for comfort, the southwest is where you will find the **Spiaggia di Citara**. Most of this sandy

Boats at Sant'Angelo

stretch is owned and operated by the Giardini Poseidon, but you can still find pockets of free access here and there. Consider biting the bullet and buying a day pass for true pleasure.

For free hot-spa action, head on down to the hidden secret of **Sorgeto**. A particular fave amongst locals, Sorgeto can be reached from the tiny village of **Panza**: directions are tricky, so be sure to ask a local for advice if you get lost. Signs exist in Panza directing you to Sorgeto; however, they look like they haven't been changed since the Roman age! Follow a series of sharp curves in the road and a long flight of stairs and you will eventually find yourself at a rocky cove. A spring gushes through the rocks and into the sea at a constant temperature of 32°C (90°F). This is a perfect locale for combining a dip in the frigid waters with a spot of soothing relaxation in the heated pools.

Proud to be Italian

The south

The sights of the southern coast of Ischia are dictated by the route of the SS270 road. Towns along this stunning route include Serrara, Fontana and Barano d'Ischia. None of the villages features anything of architectural note, but the views overlooking the sea are incredible. If you are trying to reach the summit of Monte Epomeo from the town of Fontana, follow the road marked *strada militare* and *vietato l'ingresso* (no entry) up to the top. The route is perfectly legal until you reach the bar-restaurant just before the military zone. Drive your car to this point and walk the short distance to the top. The walk should take approximately 40 minutes if you take the path to the left of the metal bar that crosses the road. From the summit there is a magnificent 360° view over Ischia.

Sant'Angelo

Ischia's most picturesque village, Sant'Angelo, is a multicoloured (ex)-fishing hamlet perched above the extraordinarily blue waters of the Mediterranean. While the town draws many international tourists – largely due to its proximity to the 2km-long beach of the **Marotti** – Sant'Angelo is largely a playground for locals. However, the beach, while still a draw, is no longer what it once was. The sea and numerous storms have eaten away much of the sand. The eastern end is reserved mostly for family-friendly fun, while geothermal activity on the western flank reserves the steamy pools for fans of heated splendour. This is where you will find the Terme Apollon (*see p118*).

Sant'Angelo is a wonderful draw for diving and underwater enthusiasts. Single dives and diving courses are available from the Roja Diving Centre, a well-run diving centre in town. All lessons are by appointment only and need to be arranged in advance of your requested date.

Roja Diving Centre

Hotel Conte, Via Nazario Sauro 54, Sant'Angelo. Tel: (081) 999 214. Fax: (081) 999 076. www.ischiadiving.it Open: By appointment only. No credit cards.

Campagnano

Just before the SS270 enters Ischia town, a quick turn-off leads to Campagnano.

There isn't all that much to warrant a visit, except for the church of **San Domenico**. Known primarily for its 19th-century majolica decorations on the façade, the church is a delightful location for a photo opportunity, thanks to its views of Ischia Porto and the Castello Aragonese on the cliffs below.

HIDDEN CORNERS

For something a little out of the ordinary, try exploring the deserted coves that line the southern cliffs of Ischia. Sant'Angelo makes for a perfect departure point if you want to enter nooks and caves that feel like they've never before been seen by human eyes (even if your boat driver has already brought twenty couples and a tour group to the same cove earlier the same day). Rent a boat-taxi from the main docks and tell them to take you to the stretch of land between the two ends of the Spiaggia dei Maronti. Be sure to negotiate your rate before you step into the boat, making sure that the quoted cost is for a round-trip adventure.

Spiaggia dei Maronti

Procida in detail

The architecture of the island is one of the most distinctive in the region. Small, multi-coloured homes rest against the tufa rock, nestled next to each other tighter than sardines in a tin. Unique to Procida are the vaulted buildings built to house boats during the winter season and enlarged over a number of generations to incorporate arches, frames, terraces, windows and other forms of exterior decoration. Examples of this quaint architecture can be seen on your arrival in Procida's **Marina di Sancio Cattolico**.

The Abbazia di San Michele Arcangelo

The main port of Procida, in existence almost since the first day the Greeks explored the area back in the 5th century BC, owes its current look to a mini-population boom in the 17th and 18th centuries. The most famous sight on the island remains the Abbey of San Michele. Dating back to 1026, the abbey has been rebuilt a number of times since the original structure was erected, and it boasts a painting by Luca Giordano of the archangel Michael. The interior is worth exploring for its large manuscript library, museum, Nativity scene and

Castello d'Avalos

labyrinthine catacombs leading to a secret chapel.
Via Terra Murata 89. Tel: (081) 896 7612. Open: Mon–Sat 9.45am–12.45pm, 3–5pm; Sun 9.45am–12.45pm. Church free. Admission charge for museum, library and catacombs.

Chiaiolella

Procida's second most popular ferry port is also its most beautiful. The marina is virtually untouched since the day the ancient structure was built, nestled in a secluded bay brimming with gardens, greenery and lemon trees. The **Vivara Nature Reserve** takes advantage of the very fertile soil of the area, displaying numerous examples of Mediterranean flora, fauna and birdlife. You can reach the reserve from Chiaiolella's marina by using a bridge that links Procida to the small island on which the park is situated.

Riserva Naturale di Vivara

No phone. Open: Mon–Sat 8.30am–noon; last entry 10am.

Castello d'Avalos

You may not be able to enter its foreboding walls today, but up until 1986 you wouldn't have wanted to. Castello d'Avalos was Italy's answer to Alcatraz – an island prison where only the worst offenders were sent. The massive structure will be the first building you see if you arrive at Procida's main port by ferry. As yet, there are no plans to open up the building as a tourist attraction.

Take in the views

HIKING THE ISLANDS

A hike through the islands of Capri, Ischia and Procida is both a popular way of getting around the tiny land masses and a great way to enjoy the archipelago's stunning views. Terra Murata, Procida's highest point, is a mere 91m (300ft) above sea level, so even the most out of shape should find a brief hike relatively easy.

Capri and Ischia make for more challenging treks. The path connecting Monte Solaro (589m, 1,930ft) to Anacapri is extremely popular and may even feel something like a busy high street on Christmas Eve if you decide to tackle it during the high season. Ischia's famed trek is the route up the extinct volcano, **Mount Epomeo** (788m, 2,580ft). Climbs to the summit usually start before dawn to ensure a view of the sunrise when you reach the top.

The Amalfi Coast and Sorrento

Just when you thought that nothing could beat the hustle and bustle of Naples, the sun-kissed splendour of Capri or the ancient mysteries of Pompeii – along comes the truly magnificent Amalfi Coast. The twists and turns of state road 163 as it leads you through this paradise suspended between the earth, sea and sky may be perilous to navigate, but most of life's best things come at a price.

Amalfi town

Until the 19th century, the towns, caves and cliffs of the Amalfi Coast were almost impossible to reach by land. Travellers looking to discover their personal Eden had to do so by hiring pack mules to take them over treacherous mountain passes. Poets, artists and writers of the Romantic era were drawn to the area for precisely this reason, and the hordes soon followed. Up until this time, life on the Amalfi Coast was filled with hardships. Pirate raids, flooding, landslides, the battering sea and isolation attacked residents on an almost daily basis. A brief period in the spotlight during the Byzantine Empire shone brightly, yet remained extinguished for centuries until its fame came from a new and highly unlikely source – northern European tourists.

Today, the Amalfi Coast is pummelled with a different sort of daily attacker – the exhaust and gridlock formed when thousands of vacationers descend on the area every weekend from April through to October. If you decide to visit during this time, then you will spend most of your day stuck behind the wheel of your car. During these long periods of inactivity, a bottle of water and constant air conditioning are musts.

Stretching from Punta della Campanella to Salerno, the Amalfi Coast can be approached from Sorrento Via Sant'Agata dei Due Golfi (between the Bay of Naples and the Gulf of Salerno), via the Colli di Chiunzi or from the south via Salerno. Whichever route you do decide to choose, you should be warned that the roads here are not for the faint-hearted. If you suffer from vertigo or a fear of sharp turns, then you might want to consider using one of the numerous tour buses that plough the route on a daily basis.

Three of the main centres along the route boast impressive tourism credentials. Visitors are drawn to Amalfi with its glorious past as a marine republic, the pastel-coloured, steep-sided fishing town of Positano and Ravello, chosen by Wagner as the setting for his opera *Parsifal*. While it may be important to check off the list, you should by no means limit your explorations to the 'big three'.

The Amalfi Coast is made to be explored, preferably at a leisurely pace. A car or coach may be necessary to discover the area's beautiful trappings, but it's the moments when you get out from behind the wheel that will truly inspire the heart.

Getting there:
From Naples airport
To Sorrento: Six coaches run in each direction every day between Naples airport and Sorrento with additional stops at Vico Equense, Piano, Meta and Sant'Agnello. The bus service is operated by Autolinee Curreri Service (*Tel: (081) 801 5420*). One-way tickets cost €5.20 and are available on the bus.

To Positano: Take the coach service to Sorrento and change for SITA (*Tel: (081) 552 2176/(089) 871 016*) local bus services.
To Amalfi: Take the coach to Sorrento and change for SITA local bus services.

By boat
To Sorrento: Linee Marittime Partenope (*Tel: (081) 807 1812/fax: (081) 532 9071*) and Alilauro (*Tel: (081) 807 3024/fax: (081) 807 3782*) run year-round hydrofoil services between Naples' Molo Beverello and Sorrento. Linee Marittime Partenope services take 35 minutes and cost €7, while Alilauro is slightly quicker at 20 minutes, costing €8.50.
To Positano: Depending on the time of year, there are one to four hydrofoils

Paradise cloister, Amalfi Cathedral

Nymph fountain

shipping passengers between the ports of Salerno, Capri, Amalfi and Positano every day. The most frequent service operates along the Amalfi–Positano route – unhelpful if you are trying to get to the coast from outside the peninsula. From June to September there is a non-stop service directly to Naples' Mergellina dock, run by Consorzio Linee Marittime (*Tel: (089) 873 301*). It is also possible to take ferry services to Positano, connecting at Capri.

To Amalfi: Regular boat services operate from Salerno and are the cheapest and quickest alternative. TraVelMar (*Tel: (089) 873 190; www.coopsantandrea.it*)

run ferries during the summer season from the Molo Manfredi dock in Salerno. LMS (*Amalfi Tel: (089) 873 301/Salerno (089) 227 979*) offer the same route, with frequent connections on to Naples.

By bus
To Sorrento: SITA is the local bus service that operates all routes out of Sorrento across the Amalfi Coast. Services on Sundays and public holidays are extremely infrequent, often stopping completely by 7pm. Ticket prices vary according to distance travelled, with no ticket more expensive than €2.12. Services run hourly between 6.35am and 8.05pm along the main Sorrento–Positano–Amalfi route.
To Positano: One bus, run by SITA, departs Naples every day from Monday to Saturday, returning in the early evening. At all other times, take the Circumvesuviana train to Meta and change for the SITA-run Sorrento–Positano–Amalfi bus.
To Amalfi: Frequent services run between Amalfi and Salerno via Positano, Agerola or Vietri. From Naples, take the Circumvesuviana train and change at Meta for the Sorrento–Amalfi bus. Times and information can be found through SITA (*Tel: (089) 871 016; www.sita-on-line.it*). Sunday services are extremely infrequent and unpredictable: avoid them if at all possible.

By car
To Sorrento: Take the SS18 coast road or the A3 motorway to Castellamare di

Stabia. At the end of the motorway, follow the SS145 southeast around the peninsula. Avoid driving if at all possible. Sundays and the summer season can choke these roads with hour-consuming traffic.

To Positano: Follow the directions to Castellamare di Stabia and turn on to the SS145. Turn onto the SS163 at Meta, 4km (2.5 miles) east of Sorrento.

To Amalfi: Leave the A3 motorway at the Angri exit and follow the signs to the Valico di Chiunzi pass and Ravello.

By train

To Sorrento: Sorrento is the terminus of the Circumvesuviana railway (*Tel: (081) 772 2444*), which runs along the Bay of Naples coast from Naples.

Services operate every 30 minutes in each direction. The last train leaves Sorrento at 11.26pm. A Naples–Sorrento ticket costs €2.84 and is valid for 3 hours.

To Positano and Amalfi: There is no Amalfi Coast train line. Travellers are advised to use other methods of transportation.

Sorrento

See p142 for more information about Sorrento.

Positano

'Positano bites deep', according to John Steinbeck. 'It is a dream place that isn't quite real when you are there and becomes beckoningly real after you have

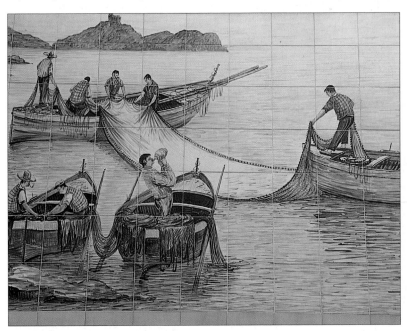

On the tiles: the fishermen of Amalfi

gone.' Steinbeck wrote these words for *Harper's Bazaar* in 1953 after visiting this pastel-toned, steep-sided town during a tour of the area. For residents during the 18th and 19th centuries, however, everyday life in Positano was all too real. Life here is and was vertical and exposed to the conditions.

Vulnerable to pirate raids and lacking any industrial base, three-quarters of the population emigrated to the United States.

The peak of respectability

What makes for a bad lifestyle makes for a great tourist destination, as evidenced

Positano, Marina Grande

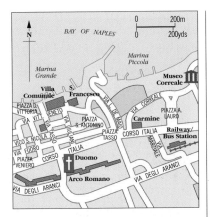

by the sheer number of tourists who visit this 'cliff with houses on it' every year. In the 1950s, Positano was a closely guarded secret, held dear by the Italian artists and writers who patronised its establishments. By 1960, the hotels, international tourists and rising starlets moved in, making it almost as popular as Capri as a place to see and be seen. If Capri was Bardot then Positano was more Garbo – famous but not wanting to make too big a statement about it. Its heyday is reflected in the modernist hotel architecture and numerous 1960s-style postcards on offer at souvenir stores throughout the village.

Foul fashions

If you've heard that Positano is a fashionable centre to make clothing purchases, then think again. While there are a number of boutiques to choose from, most of the proprietors opened their businesses during the peak of 1960s' resort-wear chic – and have yet to leave that tacky fashion era. It may be good for a last-minute purchase of a

new swimming costume, but you'd be advised to leave the multi-coloured Hawaiian dresses alone.

Navigating the town

The buildings of Positano cling precariously to the hill, climbing it in steps with the oldest structures lying in the upper section, faded to a pale pink and decorated with Baroque stuccoes. **Via Pasites**, the pedestrianised street that runs vertically through the town, is the main street you will come to know and love if a visit to the sea is in your plans. Houses seem to defy the gods in their positioning.

Cooling down

Don't worry about the baking sun; there are plenty of options available if a dip in the water is to your liking. To visit inaccessible inlets or the islands of **Li Galli**, boats are available to rent or charter at the docks. If that proves to be out of your wallet's reach, there are beaches within walking distance at **Ciumicello**, **Arienzo** and **Fornillo**. In the case of Fornillo, a direct path from the marina will lead you to the sandy stretch with its two looming watchtowers. For something a little more secluded, try the grottoes of **La Porta** – home to a number of Palaeolithic and Mesolithic ruins. In all cases, be sure to bring a bottle of water and a towel. Facilities can be limited at some locations and the sun can get extremely hot. The entire region is far from wheelchair-accessible, so be sure that you are prepared for a strenuous day of walking.

The Real Duchess of Malfi

The playwright John Webster was an extremely disturbed individual – at least, he was if you can judge him from his seminal work, *The Duchess of Malfi*. Filled with images of incest, murder, psychotic episodes, torture and a hell of a lot of blood, the play has been the plague of generations of confused students since it was written in 1613.

Set in Amalfi, the play was merely the third reincarnation of a tale that has been around since the 16th century. Originally a story written by popular Italian author Matteo Bandello in a collection of his shorter works, it was borrowed by writer William Painter for his work *Palace of Pleasure*, and in turn plagiarised yet again by Webster.

Who is she?

All fingers point to Giovanna d'Aragona (Joan of Aragon) as the unfortunate duchess in question. Member of the ruling family of Naples, Giovanna was married off to Alfonso Piccolomini, the son and heir of the Duke of Amalfi, when she was just 12. Eight years later, Alfonso died of gout and Giovanna was left a widow, pregnant with her second child.

Determined to keep some independence and romance in her life, Giovanna started a passionate affair with her steward, Antonio Bologna. Romantic liaisons with commoners were unheard of during this time and Giovanna needed to keep her lips sealed

– especially from her powerful brothers Carlo, the Marquis of Gerace in Calabria, and Lodovico, a cardinal.

Till death us do part

The couple managed to marry in secret and somehow kept the birth of two of their children away from palace spies in the pay of the brothers – until disaster finally struck. When Giovanna's clan found out about the forbidden love, Antonio fled with the two children to Ancona. Giovanna, pregnant again, followed a few months later and announced her intentions to renounce her rank and live humbly. The brothers thought otherwise and banished Antonio.

The plot thickens

It is at this point that Webster's story and the actual history of the duchess diverge. In Webster's masterpiece, the duchess is quickly set upon by palace

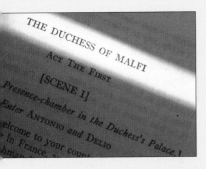

Sets and locations

To see some of the more authentic duchess-related locations, check out **Torre dello Zirro**, a crumbling watchtower that sits on a ridge between Amalfi and Atrani. Locals will tell you that it was in this spooky overlook that Giovanna and her younger children were murdered – but they are most probably wrong. A more likely spot for the dirty deed would have been in the Norman castle higher up the same ridge that called itself home to the Dukes of Amalfi until the building was dismantled in 1583. To visit both ruins, plan for an easy one-hour walk from the village of **Pontone**, accessible to Amalfi by local bus services.

spies and strangled. History, however, proves to be less tidy. Antonio and the duchess managed to live on the run throughout Italy for a number of years, until they were finally separated by a promise of safe conduct for them and their eldest son. Giovanna returned to Amalfi and effectively disappeared from all known records. Antonio survived until 1513, when he was stabbed to death by four hired assassins in a Milanese street.

Opposite: Torre di Ziro
Above: An extract from *The Duchess of Malfi*
Below: View from the Duomo, Amalfi

Museo delle Carta

Amalfi

Once a powerful maritime republic, the town of Amalfi seems to cling to both the rockface it finds itself nestled on and its 11th-century heyday when the town led Italian commerce, rivalling Venice and Genoa in port traffic and trade. Amalfi's republic took up the entire Sorrentine peninsula and much, much more. Amalfitan sailors were respected across the continent, often hired to battle on behalf of not only the republic but also neighbouring allies.

While little remains from this brief golden age a few things still hark back to the days when the town had a bustling population of over 60,000.

The Duomo di Sant'Andrea

Amalfi's main cathedral was founded in the 9th century and rebuilt many times since. While the façade and atrium date back to the late 19th century, the bronze doors that feature in the centre hark back to the year 1000 when they were cast in Constantinople. The rest of the structure is a complete mish-mash of styles, including an Italian Romanesque campanile (1276) and a divine **Chiostro del Paradiso** (paradise cloister) built for the Bishop Augustariccio in 1266 as a cemetery for the town's more fêted citizens.

From the cloister, a door leads into the **Cappella del Crocefisso**, the only part of the church to have survived relatively intact from the 12th century. Inside the chapel, glass cases hold the Duomo's treasures, including a 15th-century marble bas-relief and a bejewelled mitre made for the Anjou court of Naples in 1297.

Piazza del Duomo. Tel: (089) 871 059. Open: daily Apr–June, 2 weeks around Christmas 9am–7pm; July–Sept

THE AMALFI REGATTA

Every year, Italy's ancient maritime republics of Venice, Pisa, Genoa and Amalfi take it in turn to organise a regatta. Each town has a designated colour – blue in the case of Amalfi – and compete against each other for honour and glory. The events are preceded by a procession in period costume, bringing back memories of each city's past triumphs. The next regatta is scheduled for Amalfi in 2005 and is always held on the first Sunday in June. Hotels along the coast get fully booked up during this period and advance reservations are a necessity.

The Duomo di Sant'Andrea, Amalfi

9am–9pm; Oct, Mar 9.30am–5.15pm;
Nov–Feb 10am–1pm, 2.30–4.30pm.
Admission charge for Chiostro del
Paradiso only.

Museo delle Carta

The **Valle dei Mulini**, with Amalfi at its
heart, was the site of some of Europe's
first paper-making factories. Watermills
once dotted the landscape as they
powered the factories that made the
continent's earliest aids to record-
keeping and story-telling. One of the
original worksites, the **Palazzo Pagliara**,
has been transformed into a museum,
illustrating the history and techniques of
the trade. Go downstairs to find original
vats and machinery – some of which
date back to the Middle Ages.

High-quality paper is still produced in
the area by the **Cartiera Amatruda** and
can be purchased at boutiques and
shops throughout the town.
Palazzo Pagliara, Via delle Cartiere 23.
Tel: (089) 830 561;
www.museodellacarta.it. Open: Nov–Mar
Tue–Sun 10am–3pm; Apr–June, Oct daily
10am–6pm; July–Sept daily 10am–8pm.
Admission charge includes guided tour in
English.

Drive: The Perfect Amalfi Coast Drive

The Amalfi Coast is made to be driven, preferably by someone else. So bad is the traffic during the high season that it is often described as Europe's most picturesque car park. If you plan on driving the route, arrive early or late in the season, being sure to time it well, as most facilities, hotels, shops and restaurants close between November and February.

Allow 8 hours.

A drive along the Amalfi isn't cheap, especially if you choose to do it yourself. Non-resident parking spaces are few and far between and cost a minimum of €20 per day during high season, so plan your stops economically. Drivers will need to have a head for heights, quick reflexes and should be sure to use the helpful mirrors set up at every sharp corner along the road – and there are a lot of them.

If you prefer, you can trust your wallet, your time and your life to the expert bus drivers that traverse the route every day. In many cases, planned tours offer a hop-on, hop-off service that allows you to spend as much time as you want in any town along the coast. *This tour should take eight hours if you include stops for lunch, sunbathing, shopping and a chance to rest your legs. It begins in Sorrento at the Nastro Azzuro road*

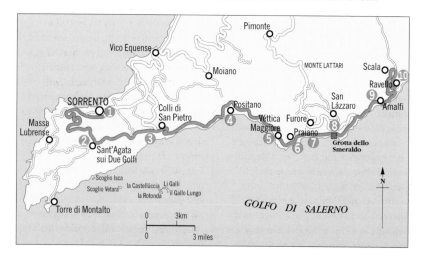

Santa Maria Assunta

(SS145). The road exits Sorrento to the west, but will eventually go eastbound, following a series of hairpin turns via Sant'Agata sui Due Golfi.

1 Sorrento

Begin your tour in Sorrento, at the western end of the Sorrentine peninsula. Be sure not to miss the **Duomo, Villa Floridiana** and various museums dedicated to chronicling Sorrento's cultural past. If at all possible, try to avoid the busy port: during high season it can sometimes resemble Benidorm with its proliferation of 'English' pubs serving plates of egg and chips to bright-red package tourists.

Drive west out of town, using the SS145. Your drive will continue along this road until you reach San Pietro where you should follow directions for the SS163.

2 Sant'Agata sui Due Golfi

A nondescript village that was once a favourite summer resort during the 18th and 19th centuries. Stop to visit the 17th-century church of **Santa Maria delle Grazie** (*open: daily 8am–1pm, 5–7pm*), featuring an immense multicoloured inlaid marble altar. Gourmets should make a reservation at the Michelin-starred Don Alfonso restaurant (*Corso Sant'Agata 13, tel: (081) 878 0026*) for its divine interpretations of local dishes. All of the garden produce is organic. The *boccadoro* (bream) comes highly recommended.

3 Between Sant'Agata and Positano: Li Galli and the San Pietro pass

The nine-mile stretch between Sant'Agata and Positano is one of the area's most difficult to manoeuvre. Steinbeck and his wife certainly thought so when they 'lay clutched in each other's arms, weeping hysterically', as their driver – in his typically Italian fashion – constantly took his eyes off the road while behind the wheel of the car to talk about the region's history.

Just off the coast are three islands, known in days of old as the home to the deadly Sirens, who lured mariners to their death with their song. Today, the islands are known as **Li Galli** and can be explored if you charter a boat from the docks at Positano.

4 Positano

This popular seaside resort is a great place to rest your legs. The main beach, **Marina Grande**, isn't exactly the most

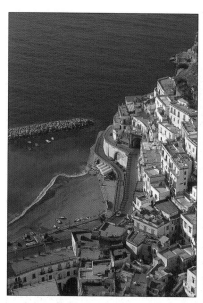

Marina di Furore

comfortable of locations to pick up a tan, filled as it is with grey pebbles, but the activity from the cafés that line the shore is addictive to watch. Colourful boats pull up to the docks throughout the day, depositing their catches straight into the hands of the numerous restaurant owners and chefs who feed their mouthwatering dishes to thousands of tourists every day.

For shopping, be sure to head for the **Piazza dei Mulini** and the **Via dei Mulini**, a narrow street that runs off the beach past the church of **Santa Maria Assunta** (*open: daily 8am–noon, 3.30–7pm*). For details of other sites, *see p133.*

5 Vettica Maggiore

This tiny village offers a beautiful beach and one of the coast's most picturesque churches, **San Gennaro**. The view from the square outside the church is simply stunning, providing perfect photo opportunities back to Positano and the rocky coast beyond.

6 Praiano

A mini-Positano with a fishing cove lying just to the east of the main part of town in the Marina di Praia. The local beach is absolutely tiny, stuck between a couple of high rock walls that allow room for only a few bar-restaurants and residences.

7 Marina di Furore

Even smaller than any of the villages previously mentioned, the Marina di Furore was recently restored with funds provided by the Campanian government. A new bar-restaurant, cinema archive, cultural centre, paper-making museum and herbarium have been opened under the auspices of the **Ecomuseo** complex.
Hours are erratic, so be sure to call ahead for details on (089) 830 4711.

8 Grotta dello Smeraldo

Amalfi's answer to Capri's famous Blue Grotto is this emerald-hued cove, located two-thirds of the way between Positano and Amalfi. A car park above the cave sits near the entrance to a lift that takes you down to a series of rowing boats that plunge under the tiny entrance. While it's not as impressive as its more famous sister in Capri, it's certainly cheaper. See if you can find the profile of former dictator Mussolini formed by the shadow of a stalagmite.

A slice of heaven: the Amalfi coastline

9 Amalfi

This former marine powerhouse may have lost some of its lustre since the 11th century, but there's still plenty to see and do. Another good place for a bite to eat and a bit of shopping, details of the more well-known local sites can be found on *pp136–7*.

10 Ravello

Ravello has drawn great artists and writers to its aristocratic old town for the best part of a century. Beginning with Richard Wagner, everyone from Franz Liszt to Virginia Woolf spent time in the romantic palazzi and hotels that dot the town. D H Lawrence is even said to have written large parts of *Lady Chatterley's Lover* in the now defunct **Hotel Rufalo**. A great place to spend the night, Ravello has plenty of other sites to explore, including the **Duomo**, **Villa Rufalo** and **Villa Cimbrone** to name a few.

Sorrento

Purists sometimes argue that Sorrento isn't the real Amalfi Coast – it's too easy to get to, too packaged and too convenient for those who love the coast's more challenging trappings – but if it's geological splendour and a steep, cliff-hugging village you're after, then you've come to the right place.

Sorrento Duomo

The central location, good infrastructure and strong transport links make Sorrento a great place from which to explore the Amalfi Coast. And if Naples' chaos and traffic are getting to you, then the laid-back lifestyles of the town will make for a delightful change-of-pace.

Inhabited since prehistoric times, the area around Sorrento has been coveted for centuries. The Greeks adored it so much that Homer sent his hero Ulysses to endure the temptations of the peninsula's siren songs in the *Odyssey*.

After the Romans moved in, they transformed Sorrento from an important Greek trading post to a holiday home-away-from-home for the empire's elite. Luxury villas sprouted up all along Sorrento's coast – a trend that remains to this day along the more picturesque and secluded roads of the area.

Sorrento maintained independence of a sort throughout the turbulent years following the fall of the Roman Empire, eventually succumbing to the Lombards and the power of neighbouring Naples in the 12th century. Unshackling Sorrento from Neapolitan influence continues to be the number one wish of all Sorrentines to this day – a wish that will ultimately never be granted.

Duomo

The original cathedral of Sorrento was rebuilt during the 15th century in the Gothic style. Fine examples of local *intarsio* (wooden inlay) work decorate the choir stalls. Of particular note is the bishop's throne dating from 1573 and constructed from a collection of marble fragments.
Corso Italia. Tel: (081) 878 2248. Open: 7.40am–noon, 4.30–8.30pm daily.

Museobottega della Tarsialignea

Situated in a restored 18th-century Palazzo, this museum holds some of Sorrento's best examples of locally-produced *intarsio* (wooden inlay) furniture. Prized by collectors, Grand Tourists and nobility alike from the mid-18th century onwards, the intricate furniture displays local craftsmanship and artistry at its finest. Old paintings and photographs of Sorrento provide additional context. The gift-shop is a must-see, riddled with modern-day interpretations of marquetry furniture. International shipping is available.
Via San Nicola 28. Tel: (081) 877 1942. www.alessandrofiorentinocollection.it. Open: Apr–Oct 9.30am–1pm, 4–8pm

Tue–Sun. Nov–Mar 9.30am–1pm, 3–7pm Tue–Sun. Admission charge.

Museo Correale di Terranova

A haphazard collection of local art and artefacts left to the town by a pair of brothers in the 1920s. The archaeological section boasts the best exhibits, including a collection of Greek and Roman marbles, Greek classical sculptures covered in inscriptions in Doric dialect, the famed Sorrento Base (1st century BC) decorated with bas-reliefs depicting the religious policy of Augustus, Attic and Campanian vases and lapidary inscriptions. There are also minor works of 17th- and 18th-century arts and paintings by the Neapolitan school.

Via Correale 50. Tel: (081) 878 1846. Open: 9am–2pm Mon, Wed–Sun. Admission charge.

Villa Fiorentino

A 19th-century villa operated by the local council. The public gardens are small, yet enjoyable on a hot summer day. The actual villa is only open on special occasions, for local art exhibitions or lectures on local history.

Corso Italia 53. Tel: (081) 533 5111. Open: 9am–1pm, 4–7pm daily.

The Marina Grande

Caserta, Salerno and Paestum

Getting out of Naples is something all residents look forward to. While they could never think of living anywhere else, all that smog, traffic and humanity are bound to get on your nerves at some time. Luckily, the countryside surrounding the city is filled with countless rural opportunities to while away lazy, summer days or fill up on culture.

Priest's gathering, Salerno

CASERTA

Caserta was an insignificant little town from its founding in the 12th century until the 1750s when the first Bourbon king Charles decided to select the area as the location of his countryside residence. Situated 20km (12 miles) north of Naples, Caserta provided a quiet spot where Charles could flee the threat of marauding Saracens and the eruptions of Vesuvius while satisfying his passion for hunting.

The Reggia

Built around four courtyards, the Reggia has 1,790 windows in 1,200 rooms, of which only a fraction are open to the public. The whole place cost around six million ducats to build and is probably the finest example of Neapolitan Baroque architecture in Italy.

The Salone delle Guardie di Corpo

This salon is the ultimate in Bourbon family self-love, filled with painted scenes taken from the lives of the Farnese family. A bust of Ferdinand I on the mantelpiece is attributed to Antonio Canova. The room next to it (the **Sala di Alessandro**) gets its name from the

fresco showing Alexander the Great's marriage to Roxana. The terrace outside was used by reigning monarchs and their families to greet the commoners with a 'royal wave'.

Eighteenth-century Royal Apartments

The Halberdiers Hall connects the upper vestibule with the Royal Apartments. Be sure to admire the ceiling decorated with a fresco painted by Domenico Mondo in 1785, entitled *The Triumph of the Bourbon Arms*. The furniture and decoration of the rooms act as a veritable museum documenting the development of craftsmanship and style from the Rococo period to the neoclassical.

The Appartamento Vecchio

Each of the first four rooms in this series of apartments is dedicated to the four seasons, beginning with *primavera* (spring). But it's the interiors that have to be seen to be believed. The walls of the *estate* (summer) room are covered in San Leucio silk and topped off with a priceless chandelier made from Murano glass, while the *autunno* dining room has stunning frescoes of Bacchus and Ariadne.

The Sala del Trono (Throne Room)

Ambassadors were received and ambitious balls held in this large 19th-century salon. Decorated by Gaetano Genovese in 1844, the room is lit by 14 Bohemian glass and bronze lamps and has a throne of carved and gilded wood. Empty today, the room was originally filled with elegant French furniture.

Ferdinand II's bedchamber lies close to the throne room, containing an early roll-top desk. The adjoining bathroom and study belonged to Joaquin Murat, brother-in-law to Napoleon and King of Naples from 1808 to 1816. The bedchamber is in the French Empire style, filled with mahogany and bronze inlay furniture. Note Murat's initials carved into the chairs – a symbol of his well-known and well-documented narcissism.

The Biblioteca (Library)

The library houses a collection of over 10,000 volumes distributed over a series of several rooms. Next to the library is a Nativity scene containing over 1,200 figures made by 18th-century craftsmen. The clothing on all of the figures was

Arco di Traiano

made by the queen and her ladies-in-waiting. The glass display cases lie above what was formerly the palace stage before the much grander Court theatre was built.

Museo dell'Opera

Students of architecture will love the displays and records containing documents and plans tracing the history of the palace's construction.

Reggia di Caserta (Palazzo Reale)

Via Douet 2. Tel: Reggia (0823) 321 400/0823 447 147. Museo dell'Opera tel: (0823) 332 1400. Open: Reggia Tue–Sun 8.30am–7.30pm. Museo Tue–Sun 9am–1pm. Parco Tue–Sun 9am–1hr before sunset. Admission charge.

Getting there

By car

Take the A1 motorway from Naples, exiting at Caserta Sud.

By train

Frequent services run to Caserta from Naples' Stazione Centrale. The journey takes about 30 minutes, followed by a 5-minute walk to the Reggia.

By bus

CTP (*Tel: (081) 504 8150*) run from Piazza Garibaldi in Naples to Caserta and Capua. Look for buses marked *per autostrada*: these services take the motorway and cut journey times in half.

SALERNO

Salerno proper owes its roots to the Roman town of Salernum which was founded on this site in 194 BC. The city didn't hit its stride until the dawn of the Lombards and (especially) the Normans, who made Salerno their capital in 1077.

This boom period didn't turn to bust until the 13th century, with the rise of the Angevins who favoured neighbouring Naples as their administrative head-quarters. Salernians still haven't really got over this fact and hold bitter feelings in their hearts for their more prosperous Neapolitan cousins.

Duomo

Each major city in Italy needs a Duomo and Salerno is no exception. Dedicated to the town's patron saint, St Matthew, the Duomo dominates the centre of the old city. Built after the Norman conquest of the town in the 11th century, the Duomo was constructed to celebrate victory over the Lombards. Designed in the Romanesque style, the exterior was heavily altered in the 18th century to accommodate the Baroque fashion during an era of major post-earthquake reconstruction. Subsequent restorations have reverted back to the original Romanesque look, but elements of the 'update' remain.
Piazza Alfano 1. Tel: (089) 231 387. Open: daily 7.30am–8pm.

Museo Archeologico Provinciale

Situated in the former abbey of San Benedetto, this museum is dedicated to the Etruscan influence on the city and the numerous chance finds that have occurred in the area over the past couple of centuries. One of the highlights of

Salerno cathedral

the collection is a 1st-century head of Apollo made from bronze that was found in the Gulf of Salerno in 1930.
Via San Benedetto 28. Tel: (089) 231 135. Open: Mon–Sat 9.30am–7.30pm; Sun 9am–1.30pm.

Getting there

By car

Salerno is located directly on the A3 motorway 55km south from Naples.

By train

Regular services run on the Naples–Reggio–Calabria line from Naples' Stazione Centrale. Journey time is approximately 45 minutes.

By bus

SITA (Tel: (089) 405 145; www.sita-on-line.it) runs regular services from Naples' Piazza Municipia.

IL PARCO

Luigi Vanvitelli not only designed the massive palace, he was also in charge of landscaping the immense gardens surrounding the palace – and what a job he made of it. One of the last examples of a regimented garden in the Italian style, the central axis is designed on descending levels, each littered with pools, fountains and ornamental sculptures. The *pièce de resistance* is the **Grande Cascata** waterfall. Almost 80m high, the Cascata (also known as the Fountain of Diana) acts as the park's central feature. Located next to this is the **English Garden**, one of the first of its kind in Italy. Landscaping work on the English Garden began in 1768 after the idea was suggested to Queen Maria Carolina by her very close 'friend' Lord Hamilton.

PAESTUM

The ruins of Paestum date back to 600 BC when Greeks from Sybaris founded a large town on the plains that lie on the left bank of the river Sele. The colony, known as Poseidonia, featured a traditional grid-pattern layout of massive temples, and a vast agora (market) testifying to the area's prosperity. Don't miss the adjoining Archaeological Museum, which has some excellent displays of Greek sculpture and finds from local necropolises.

Temple of Neptune

Roman Paestum

Poseidonia became a Roman colony in 273 BC and was renamed Paestum. Paestum took to Romanisation easily, and flourished briefly until the Second Punic War brought soldiers carrying malaria into the city gates. Residents bravely battled the disease throughout the 1st century AD, until the disease finally took its toll and the city was abandoned.

Agora

This is located south of the main entrance to the site on a plateau. Excavations underneath revealed two Greek structures, the **Underground Sacellum** and the **Ekklesiasterion**. Built in 470 BC, the Ekklesiasterion was the government centre of Poseidonia. Citizens would gather to pass laws and elect local magistrates. When the Romans arrived, democracy was thrown out the window and the structure was filled in.

The Sacellum was more religious in tone, built to house the symbolic sepulchre of the town's hero. It was buried as a 'lucky charm' or shrine to protect the city from evil.

The Forum

A Roman addition, the Forum was used as the city's public square. One of the most complete ancient structures in Italy, the Forum contains an amphitheatre, town treasury, Italic Temple and a number of *Tabernae* (stores).
Via Magna Grecia. Tel: (082) 881 1016. Open: Site daily 9am–1hr before sunset. Museum daily 8.45am–7pm. Closed 1st & 3rd Mon of the month. Admission charge.

Getting there

By car

Take the A3 motorway south from Naples to Salerno. From Salerno, follow the SS18 coast road south to Paestum.

By train

The Naples–Reggio–Calabria line from Naples' Stazione Centrale stops at Paestum. The main train station is called Capaccio Scalo. Buses run infrequently from the station to the ruins. Try and board a train stopping at the much smaller Paestum station, 10 minutes by foot away from the site. Trains run to and from this station much less frequently.

By bus

Hourly services are run by CSTP (*Tel: (089) 252 228* or *(089) 487 286*) from Salerno's Piazza della Concordia. *For bus services to Salerno, see p146.*

Shopping

Naples may not be a fashion mecca like Milan, but there are still plenty of opportunities to blow your wallet. Retailers in the city follow old-fashioned sales methods, usually choosing not to pay the slightest attention to you until you actually purchase something at the counter. And even then, ringing in the item is just such hard work!

Market-fresh fruit and veg

If a shop has display shelves, be sure to ask a shop assistant for help or you may be escorted out of the building. If you speak Italian, it will help you immeasurably. Speak with a Neapolitan accent and you may even be given good customer service.

Shopping hours

Almost all shops in Naples close for lunch from 1.30–4.30pm. Some clothes and food shops open on Sunday mornings, particularly around Montesanto and Centro Storico. Certain food shops close on Thursday afternoons in winter. The majority of non-food shops close on Monday mornings. Saturday afternoons during summer are also often a no-go time. In August, schedules get thrown out the window as locals abandon the city for their annual vacation.

What to buy

Naples is renowned for a number of items, both edible and not. This town wasn't a courtly capital and artistic headquarters for nothing! Whether you're a bibliophile who loves to collect antiquarian books, a foodie who devours antipasti at every opportunity

or a fashionista who loves Italian duds, then you've come to the right place. Bargains are available all year round, but the best deals are found during the sale seasons of January, February and August.

Be sure to try on all items of clothing before you buy them. US and UK sizes printed on the labels often differ greatly from the actual truth, and refund policies are non-existent in almost all Neapolitan shops.

Pickpockets ahead!

To avoid being targeted by Naples' deadly-accurate pickpockets, avoid shopping between the hours of 6pm and 8pm. Workers going home after a long day crowd the streets along with locals out for a stroll, transforming pavements into a mess of elbows and shopping bags. Take out your wallet or make a big purchase and you can be sure it will soon find its way into someone else's pocket.

Antiquarian books and prints
Bowinkel

The most respected dealer of period prints and photographs in town. *Piazza dei Martiri 24, Chiaia. Tel: (081) 764 4344.*

Colonnese

Publishers and collectors of works both old and new. Speciality subjects include the arts, magic and history. A great place to find distinctive Neapolitan tarot and playing cards.
Via Carlo Poerio 17, Chiaia.
Tel: (081) 764 0770.

Books

Liberia Feltrinelli

The biggest bookshop in Naples. Go downstairs to find works in English. Theatre and concert bookings are available on the first floor.
Piazza dei Martiri/Via Santa Caterina a Chiaia 23, Chiaia. Tel: (081) 240 5411.

An antique-hunter's paradise

Ceramics
La Bottega della Ceramica
Beautiful ceramics collected from across southern Italy. Prices are very reasonable.
Via Carlo Poerio 40, Chiaia.
Tel: (081) 764 2626.

Department stores
La Rinascente
Naples' most upmarket department store, with a good selection of underwear and perfumes. Housed in a former palazzo on the Via Toledo.
Via Toledo 340, Toledo.
Tel: (081) 411 511.

Fashion
Eddie Monetti
Conservative yet well-crafted pieces that are both timeless and fashionable. The quality is impeccably high. So are the prices. Womenswear is located a few doors down in the Piazzetta Santa Caterina.
Via dei Mille 45, Chiaia.
Tel: (081) 407 064.

Fusaro
Fine, hand-tailored shirts. You pick the collars, cuffs, buttons and fronts.
Via Toledo 280, Toledo.
Tel: (081) 420 7014.

Marinella
The finest purveyor of men's accessories, watches, scents and jewellery in the city for over 80 years. A made-to-measure tie from Marinella is a sign that you have arrived.
Riviera di Chiaia 287A, Chiaia.
Tel: (081) 245 1182.

Maxi Ho
The best selection of fashion-forward and avant-garde pieces for women in Naples. A far cry from the traditionally tailored clothing available at most other boutiques.
Via Nisco 20, Chiaia. Tel: (081) 414 721.

Food and drink
Antiche Delizie
The best mozzarella in town. Also the best meat, cheese, preserves and antipasti. Wines and fresh pasta dishes are also on offer.
Via Pasquale Scura 14, Toledo.
Tel: (081) 551 3088.

Jewellery
Arte in Oro
Fabulous copies of original Roman jewellery. Antique items are also available.
Via B Croce 20, Centro Storico.
Tel: (081) 551 6980.

Galotta
Exclusive pieces made by local craftsmen.
Via Chiaia 139, Chiaia.
Tel: (081) 401 954.

Shoes and leather
Fratelli Tramontano
Neapolitan craftsmanship in the form of fine, handmade shoes and bags. Expensive, but worth every penny.
Via Chiaia 142–143, Royal.
Tel: (081) 668 572.

ON CAPRI
Designer shops line **Via Vittorio Emanuele** and **Via Camerelle**. Big

names include Gucci, Fendi and Ferragamo. For something a little more native, try the following options:

La Conchiglia
A local publisher with a catalogue of books about Capri's history and residents. Some of the works have been translated into English.
Via Camerelle 18. Tel: (081) 837 8199.

Limoncello di Capri
The shop where it all started. If you're looking for the best example of the local liqueur, then come to the place where they first created it.
Via Roma 79. Tel: (081) 837 5561.
www.limoncello.com

Sara Aprea
Vases, Murano glass and delicate ceramics. The shop also acts as a pottery workshop.
Via La Botteghe 6. Tel: (081) 837 0165.

IN SORRENTO
Fattoria Terranova
Fine, locally made produce. An excellent place to stock up on nibbles for a drive along the Amalfi Coast.
Piazza Tasso 16. Tel: (081) 878 1263.

Primo Piano Oggetti
Original ceramic tiles, plates and cups. A nice change from the usual tourist tat.
Corso Italia 161. Tel: (081) 807 2927.

Salvatore Gargiulo
Sorrento's best furniture workshop, specialising in marquetry and wooden inlay which is famous throughout the region.

Via Fuoro 33. Tel: (081) 878 2420
www.gargiuloinlaid.it

IN AMALFI
Antichi Sapori d'Amalfi
Limoncello and fruit liqueurs aplenty. All are locally produced in small batches and are extremely potent.
Piazza Duomo 39. Tel: (089) 872 062.

Pasticceria Andrea Pansa 1830
Wonderful pastry shop specialising in anything flavoured with lemons.
Piazza del Duomo 40. Tel: (089) 871 065.

La Scuderia del Duca
Amalfi's best handmade paper shop. Available by the sheet or in books and reams.
Largo Cesareo Console 8.
Tel: (089) 872 976.

Football shirts are a popular buy

One of Naples' most pleasurable shopping experiences is a visit to a market. Pulsing with energy, this is definitely not a challenge for the faint of heart. If you thought that the Harrods Christmas sales could get nasty, then you have never tried to snag a bargain in this town. To tackle the markets effectively, banish all thoughts of order and queuing. If you see something you like, then grab it before someone else does. If there is a long wait, take matters into your own hands by jostling for position – preferably using your elbows, feet and any other object you can find other than your fists. Even little old ladies get in on the act – in fact, they use their perceived frailness to their advantage! So keep your wallet firmly hidden, check your credit cards at the door (trust me, you won't be needing them) and prepare yourself for a fight. Round one begins now.

Bancarelle a San Pasquale

Edible goodies are sold along Via San Pasquale and Via Carducci. Things to wear are available in stalls on Via Imbriani. Good for fish, fruit, vegetables, underwear and cheap jewellery.
Via Carducci, Via Imbriani and Via San Pasquale, Chiaia. Open: Mon–Wed, Fri, Sat 8am–2pm. Closed Aug. Bus C25. Tram 1, 4.

Fiera Antiquaria Napoletana

A treasure trove of antiques both real and fake. If one of Naples' crumbling villas is emptying their stock out, then chances are you'll find the stuff here.
Villa Comunale, Chiaia. Open: From 7am last Sun of the month and occasional Sat. Closed: Aug. Bus C25. Tram 1, 4.

La Pignasecca

One of the city's oldest markets packed, with fish, vegetables, deli nibbles, perfumes, clothes, linens and kitchenware. Nothing is particularly five-star, but it's the atmosphere that makes it all worth it.
Via Pignasecca. Open: daily 8am–1pm. Funicular Montesanto to Montesanto. Metro Montesanto. Bus 24, 105, R1.

Mercatino di Antignano

The best place for things for the home. Tons of kitchenware, linens and towels at cut-rate prices. Goods are both second-hand and end-of-the-line markdowns.
Between Via Mario Fiore and Piazza degli Artisti, Vomero. Open: Mon–Sat 8am–1pm. Closed Aug. Metro Medaglio D'Oro. Bus R1.

Mercatino di Poggioreale

Shoes, shoes and more shoes. Check for quality before you buy.
Via M di Caramanico, off Via Nuova Poggioreale. Open: Mon, Fri–Sun 8am–2pm. Closed: Aug. Bus C61, C62. Tram 1, 4.

Mercatino di Posillipo

More clothes, shoes and bags. The early bird definitely gets the fake Fendi.
Viale Virgilio, Posillipo. Open: Thur 8am–2pm. Closed: Aug. Bus C27.

Mercatino di Resina

A massive flea market packed with goods taken from homes across the Bay area. You want a used accordion? They've got it! An original pair of opera glasses? Try selecting from six possible stalls! How about a couple of centuries-old linen nighties? Why not three? Situated in Ercolano, a visit here makes a great day out when combined with a visit to the site of Herculaneum.

Via Pougliano, Ercolano. Open: daily 8am–1pm. Closed Aug. Circumvesuviana rail to Ercolano.

Mercato delle Pulci

Old knick-knacks, small furnishings and ceramics. Most of it is trash, but you'll occasionally find the odd gem or two.
Via de Roberto, Poggioreale. Open: Sun 8am–1pm. Closed: Aug. Bus 191.

Opposite, above and below: You can find almost anything at a Naples market

Jazz club

Entertainment

When it comes to entertainment, Naples shouldn't fail to fulfil all your expectations – and more. Sure, you may have to book well ahead for some of the big-ticket offerings at the San Carlo, but you won't be disappointed if a streetside serenade is all you can afford. The city that brought us Commedia Dell'Arte and the movie magic of Sophia Loren is culturally alive. From visually vibrant art to momentous music, Naples has it all.

Theatres

Bellini

A sumptuous theatre that stages prose, international musicals, dance and concerts. Plays are usually performed in Italian.

Catch a flick at the Modernissimo cinema

Via Conte di Ruvo 14–19.
Tel: (081) 549 9688. www.teatrobellini.it

Mercadante

A beautiful theatre that has been showing performances since 1779. The acoustics are uniformly awful.
Piazza Municipio 1.
Tel: (081) 551 3396.
www.caspi.it/mercadante

Le Nuvole

Kids' shows in a theatre situated in the heart of the Edenlandia amusement park.
Viale Kennedy 26. Tel: (081) 239 5653. www.lenuvole.com

San Carluccio

A tiny space used primarily for cabaret and small-scale local productions.
Via San Pasquale a Chiaia 49.
Tel: (081) 405 000.

Teatro di San Carlo

Naples' *pièce de resistance.* Second to only Milan's La Scala as a home to opera. The San

Carlo ballet company also performs on this stage.
Via San Carlo 98F. Tel: (081) 797 2412.
www.teatrosancarlo.it

Teatro Nuovo
A modern theatre built over the site of one of the city's oldest theatres. New and international theatre is the focus.
Via Montecalvario 16. Tel: (081) 425 958.
www. teatronuovo.com

Totò
A venue for old-style stand-up and cabaret. Traditional farce and music-hall style comedy keeps the box office tills full.
Via Frediano Cavara 12E. Tel: (081) 564 7525. www.teatrototo.com

Summer music festivals
When the summer weather gets too hot to bear, concerts move outdoors. A couple of festivals to take note of include:

Concerti al tramonto
Fondazione Axel Munthe, Villa San

Michele, Anacapri. Tel: (081) 837 1401.
www.sanmichele.org/indexEN.html

Festival Musicale di Villa Rufolo
Società dei concerti di Ravello, Via Trinità 3, Ravello. Tel: (089) 858 149.
www.ravello.info

Galleries
The Neapolitan modern art scene has seen something of a revival since 1993. Under former mayor Antonio Bassolino, the city commissioned a number of public works, specifically for the new underground system. Art galleries have sprouted up to accommodate this new-found interest. Some of the better galleries include:

404 arte contemporanea
A tiny exhibition space hosting up-and-coming artists. The owner has a wealth of knowledge on what's hot in the city.
Via Ferrara 4. Tel: (081) 554 6139.

Archivio Fotografico Pariso
A historical archive and permanent

Look out for summer music festivals

exhibition dedicated to 19th-century Neapolitan photography.
Gallery: Porticato San Francesco di Paola 10/Photo archive: Piazza Carolina 10. Tel: (081) 764 5122.

Framart Studio
A well-established gallery hosting the best in avant-garde.
Via Nuova San Rocco 62.
Tel: (081) 741 4672.

Galleria Scognamiglio
Personal exhibitions by Italian and foreign artists.
Via M d'Ayala 6. Tel: (081) 400 871.

Studio Trisorio
The most active gallery in town, dealing in contemporary international art.
Riviera di Chiaia 215. Tel: (081) 414 306.

Cinemas
Naples may be home to Sophia Loren, but, unlike her, no cinema-goer will ever learn anything but Italian, since almost all films are dubbed. Look for the letters VO (*versione originale*) for English-language screenings.

Abadir
One of two cinemas in town that screens movies in their original language. Most of the selection is standard Hollywood fare.
Via Paisiello 35. Tel: (081) 578 9447.

Amedeo
The other cinema offering English-language films. Once again, you'll have to make do with American blockbusters.
Via Martucci 69. Tel: (081) 680 266.

Modernissimo
An arthouse cinema with children's films, restored classics and European oddities.
Via Cisterna dell'Olio 59.
Tel: (081) 551 1247.

Entrance to the Modernissimo

Contemporary art

Children

Naples is a child-friendly city in name only. While perfect strangers will dote all over your little angels at every opportunity, the streets are certainly not made for their entertainment. If you were ever told by your parents about the days when a stick and a ball was all that was needed for hours of entertainment then you can see it in practice in Neapolitan streets.

Edenlandia

Beaches

City beaches are decidedly unclean and should be avoided at all costs. Your best bet is to head out of town to the Amalfi Coast or to the outlying islands. The beaches here are small and rocky, and you will have to keep watch of your children at all times.

Funfair

Edenlandia is a traditional funfair with a host of ageing thrill-rides. Your kids will love it.
Viale Kennedy, Fuorigrotta. Tel: (081) 239 4800. Open: Apr, May Tue–Fri 2–8pm, Sat, Sun 10.30am–midnight; June, Sept Mon–Fri 5pm–midnight, Sat,

Keep the kids happy, splashing around in the water

Sun 10.30am–midnight; July, Aug Mon–Sat 5pm–midnight, Sun 10.30am–midnight; Oct–Mar Sat, Sun 10.30am–midnight.

Museums

Few museums offer the type of hands-on displays kids know and love. Some of the more interesting displays from a child's perspective are at the Musei inter-dipartimentali for fossils and stuffed animals, the Nativity crib in the Certosa di San Martino (*see p46*), the mediaeval works and fortifications in the Castel dell'Ovo (*see p38*) and the dungeons of the Castel Nuovo (*see pp38–9*). Of note is the **Città della Scienza** (*Via Coroglio 104. Tel: (081) 372 3728. Open: Tue–Sat 9am–5pm, Sun 10am–7pm*), a child-friendly museum of attractions, many of which are hands-on. Also inside is a Planetarium with showings throughout the day.

Outside the city, your best bets are the ancient ruins of Pompeii, the sulphurous crater of Vesuvius and the Pietrarsa railway museum (*see p91*) – even if you aren't a fan of trains, it's still worth a visit.

Public parks

For a spot of outdoor play in the heart of town, take your children to the Villa Comunale or Villa Floridiana – but they won't feature any of the playground options your kids may be searching for. For the usual set of swings and slides, you'll have to head further afield to the **Parco del Poggio** in the northwest of town.

Shopping

If you need children's clothes while in Naples, then department stores and markets are your best resource. To keep your kids occupied, head over to Feltrinelli (*see p149*), the only shop in town with a selection of reading material in English.

SUGAR AND SPICE

Neapolitan children get away with murder. Your kids will too. On public transport, grannies lacking both their limbs and suffering from heart disease would rather die than let your perfectly healthy child stand up during the journey. If they offer up their seat you should go ahead and take it. They will be offended if you don't.

In public places, children are perfectly allowed to whinge, scream, yell and demand whatever they want. Even if you go to the smartest restaurant in town and your child starts resembling Linda Blair from *The Exorcist*, he or she will be doted on all the more.

Sport and Leisure

Italians are passionate about sport, especially football. Tickets to major matches can be like gold dust but are well worth the trip, if only to see the carnival of activity that goes on at every match. There are plenty of opportunities to participate in sports in Naples. From bowling and sailing to watersports and tennis, there are facilities to suit all tastes.

Shrine to El Diego

SPECTATOR SPORTS
Football (Soccer)
Italian football is like a religion unto itself, and Neapolitans worship at the feet of their local team, Napoli SSC. The gods have not been kind to the players recently, yet fans continue to flock to matches whenever there is a fixture.
Stadio San Paolo is where all the action takes place, and matches are played on alternate Sundays between September and June. Kick-off can be any time between 2.30pm and 4.30pm. Check the time when you buy your ticket. Tickets for all matches (when available) can be bought at the club's main outlet, Azzuro Service.
Azzuro Service *Via F Galeota 17, Fuorigrotta. Tel: (081) 593 4001.*
Stadio San Paolo *Piazzale Tecchio, Fuorigrotta. Tel: (081) 593 3223.*

SPORTING ACTIVITIES
Bowling
Bowling Oltremare
A 20-lane bowling alley located next to the zoo and Edenlandia funfair. Ping-pong tables are also available for hire by the hour.

Viale Kennedy 12, Fuorigrotta. Tel: (081) 624 444. Open: Sun 9am–2am daily.

Gyms
Athena
The usual gym equipment, as well as aerobics classes, bicycles, weights and martial arts. There is also a Turkish bath, sauna, bar and squash court. Racquets are available for hire.
Via dei Mille, Chiaia. Tel: (081) 407 334. Open: Oct–Mar Mon–Fri 8am–10.30pm, Sat 9am–6pm, Sun 9am–noon; Apr–Sept Mon–Fri 8am–10.30pm, Sat 9am–4.30pm.

Bodyguard
Weights, bicycles, running machines and a sauna. Aerobics and dance classes are also on offer.
Via Torrione San Martino 45, Vomero. Tel: (081) 558 4551. Open: Mon–Fri 10am–11pm, Sat 11am–7pm. Closed 2 weeks in Aug.

Jogging
There are no official jogging tracks in the city. Popular locations for a run include the seafront from Castel dell'Ovo to Mergellina, the upper

reaches of Via Petrarca, the roads around Capo Posillipo and the gardens surrounding the Museo di Capodimonte.

Swimming pools
Collana
A city-owned indoor pool measuring 25m × 8m. Admission includes access to the sundeck and deck chairs.
Via Rossini, Vomero. Tel: (081) 560 1988. Open: July, Aug Mon–Sat 9.30am–2.30pm (last ticket 1.30pm), 3.30–9pm (last ticket 7pm), Sun 9am–4pm. Closed Sept–June.

Scandone
Another public swimming pool for the masses. Under-12s pay half-price.
Viale dei Giochi del Mediterraneo, Fuorigrotta. Tel: (081) 570 2636.

Open: July, Aug daily 9am–7pm. Closed Sept–June.

Tennis
Tennis Club Mostra
Four clay courts surrounded by orange trees in the western suburbs. The club can usually arrange a partner to play with you. Racquets are available for hire.
Via Terracina, Fuorigrotta. Tel: (081) 239 0444. Open: daily 8am–8pm.

Tennis San Domenico
Five floodlit clay courts located under a flyover. Racquets are available free of charge. A separate gym for weight training and aerobics adjoins the club.
Via San Domenico 64, Vomero Alto. Tel: (081) 645 660. Open: Mon–Fri 7am–10pm, Sat 7am–8pm, Sun 7am–6pm.

Posing on blades

Food and Drink

Neapolitan cuisine is based on the three Ps: pizza, pasta and *pomodoro* (tomato). While living next to Vesuvius certainly has its drawbacks, one of the main benefits is the fact that the entire region of Campania is extremely fertile. The volcanic ash has transformed the soil into a rich resource for diverse agriculture, and some of Italy's finest fruits and vegetables can be found on farms throughout the area.

Seafood special

GLOSSARY OF FOOD AND DRINK

Carne al Ragù: A typical Sunday meal of meat rolls served in a tomato sauce.

Casatiello: A traditional country-style pie, made at Easter and filled with a salami, cheese and egg stuffing.

Cheeses and dairy produce: The best local cheese is *mozzarella*, which was originally made from buffalo milk. *Fiordilatte* and *treccia di mozzarella* (made from cow's milk) are excellent when served with tomatoes and basil. There are many types of *provolone* and *scamorza* cheeses (stuffed and smoked), depending on their origin. Fresh *ricotta* is used for both savouries and sweet pastries. Grated *parmesan* is often used to flavour pasta dishes.

Coffee: Neapolitan coffee is lighter than espresso and tastes good even when re-heated. The coffee is made in a typical Neapolitan coffee maker consisting of two metal cylinders (one with a spout) and a central container to hold finely ground roast coffee.

Frutti di Mare: Seafood served with *spaghetti* or *risotto*. It can be fried or grilled when prepared and is usually made up of all different kinds of seafood fished from along the coast.

Parmagiana di Melanzane: Layers of aubergines, tomato sauce, mozzarella, grated Parmesan and basil. Courgettes may also be used.

Pasta e Fagioli: A simple dish of pasta and beans.

Pastries: Typical local delicacies include *sfogliatelle* (pastries filled with ricotta, sugar and candied fruit), *pastiera* (a special Easter or Christmas cake), *struffoli* (pastries with honey and fruit, usually served at Christmas) and *zeppole* (light doughnuts served during the feast of San Giuseppe).

Pesce all'Acqua Pazza: Fresh fish cooked in water with tomatoes, garlic and parsley.

Sartù di Riso: A rice mould served with garnishes.

Spaghetti con le Vongole: A typical first course of spaghetti with fresh clams. The sauce can be based either on olive oil or on tomato with parsley.

Wines and drinks: The white *Lacrima Christi* wine, made for centuries by monks on the slopes of Vesuvius, goes well with fish dishes. *Greco di Tufo* is another good possibility, while *Limoncello* is a locally produced lemon-flavoured liqueur.

Where to eat

Food is an important feature in the daily life of your typical Neapolitan. As such, there is a plethora of high-quality restaurants to choose from – as long as you like Italian cuisine. If at first glance a dining spot seems run-down and cramped, you shouldn't let that dissuade you. Menus may be in dialect or dishes named after a close family relation, but you can easily overcome the problems of translation by taking a look at what others around you are eating. If you like the look of something, point to it when the waiter approaches. The results will invariably tantalise your taste buds to the point of saying 'That's amore!'

Meal prices

Prices at Italian restaurants can vary widely in price. You will find everything from value-for-money finds to high-class dining blowouts. Prices in this guide are subject to fluctuation and should only be used as a rough guide.

*	Under €60
**	€60–€80
***	€80–€100
****	Over €100

Coffee, a snack and a chat

Naples is in love with European café culture. There are quite simply hundreds of excellent small cafés, from the traditional to the trendy, where you can have a great coffee and a pastry or two. Overleaf are just a few of the recommended establishments.

Luscious Limoncello

You can't have an Italian meal without pasta

Bar Mexico
Piazza Dante 86. Tel: (081) 549 9330.
Open: Mon–Sat 7.30am–8.30pm.

Caffè dell'Epoca
Via Constantinopoli 82. Tel: (081) 402
794. Open: Mon–Sat 7.30am–10pm,
Sun 7.30am–2pm.

Gambrinus
Via Chiaia 1–2. Tel: (081) 417 582.
Open: daily 8am–1.30am.

La Caffettiera
Piazza Vanvitelli 10. Tel: (081) 578 2592.
Open: Mon–Fri 7am–midnight.

Traditional Neapolitan food
Cantina della Sapienza*
The best Neapolitan home cooking in
the city (if you don't get an invite into a
private home, that is). Order any of the
traditional dishes and you won't go far
wrong.
Villa della Sapienza 40. Tel: (081) 459
078. Open: Mon–Sat noon–3.30pm.
Closed Aug.

D'Angelo Santa Caterina***
The perfect place for a romantic dinner.
While the food is invariably excellent,
the jasmine-filled surroundings with a
view over the city make dining all the
more incredible.
Via Aniello Falcone 203. Tel: (081)
578 9772. Open: Mon, Wed–Sat
7.30–10.30pm; Sun 1–3.30pm,
7.30–10.30pm. Closed 2 weeks in Aug.

Giuseppone a Mare***
For a truly blowout meal, book your
table here. Perfect meals, perfect views,
attentive service – it's all here.
Via F Russo 13. Tel: (081) 769 1384.
Open: Tue–Sat noon–3.30pm,
7.30–11.30pm; Sun 1–3.30pm.
Closed 2 weeks in Aug.

La Cantina del Sole**
An intimate dining spot, featuring
recipes that date back to the 17th and
18th centuries. Great if you want to try
delicious dishes that you won't find on
any other menu in the city.
Via Paladino 3. Tel: (081) 552 7312.
Open: Tue–Sat 7pm–midnight; Sun
1–3.30pm, 7pm–midnight. Closed Aug.

La Cantinella***
A temple of food. Elaborate fish dishes
are the most noteworthy items on the
menu.

Neapolitan café culture

Via Cuma 42. Tel: (081) 764 8684.
Open: May–Aug Mon–Sat 12.30–3pm,
7.30–11.30pm. Sept–Apr Mon–Sat
12.30–3pm, 7.30–11.30pm, Sun
7.30–11.30pm. Closed 2 weeks in Aug.

Osteria da Tonino*

The busiest *osterie* in town, thanks to the
antics of the husband-and-wife team
who run the joint. Food is tasty and
filling, if a little basic.
Via Santa Teresa a Chiaia 47. Tel: (081)
421 533. Open: Oct–May Mon–Wed
12.30–4pm, Thur–Sat 12.30–4pm,
8–11pm. June, July, Sept Mon–Sat
12.30–4pm. Closed Aug.

Simposium*

Traditional Neapolitan recipes featuring
period recipes accompanied by music
and entertainment appropriate to the
cuisine. Meals are served at communal
banqueting tables. By appointment only.
Via B Croce 38. Tel: (081) 551 8510.
Open: Fri 9pm–midnight; Sat 1–4pm,
9pm–midnight; Sun 1–4pm.

Zi Teresa**

Naples' favourite haunt for special
gatherings. Zi Teresa has been dishing
up good, solid food to the locals since
1916.
Borgo Marinaro 1. Tel: (081) 764 2565.

Open: Tue–Sat 1–3.30pm, 8–11.30pm;
Sun 1–4pm. Closed lunch 1 week in Aug.

Amalfi
'A Paranza**
Exquisite seafood dishes. The octopus
comes highly recommended. Go for the
house white wine, produced just down
the street in Ravello.
Traversa Dragone 2. Tel: (089) 871 840.
Open: Aug daily 12.30–3pm,
7.30pm–midnight. Sept–July Mon,
Wed–Sun 12.30–3pm, 7.30pm–midnight.
Closed 2 weeks in Dec.

Da Gemma***
A historic and popular venue
specialising in good local cuisine. Try
the *melanzane in salse di cioccolato*
(aubergines in chocolate sauce) for a
truly inspiring end to a fabulous meal.

Via Fra' Gerardo Sasso 10. Tel: (089) 871
345. Open: Aug Mon, Tue, Thur–Sun
7.30–10.30pm. Mid-Feb–July, Sept–mid
Jan Mon, Tue, Thur–Sun 12.30–2.30pm,
7.30–10.30pm. Closed mid-Jan–mid-Feb.

La Caravella****
Amalfi's best restaurant, offering
incredible seafood and an extensive wine
list. The chefs pull out all the stops to
make a meal here an experience you'll
remember for a lifetime.
Via Matteo Camera 12. Tel: (089) 871
029. Open: Mon, Wed–Sun noon–2.30pm,
7.30–10.30pm. Closed mid-Nov–Dec.

Capri
Da Gemma**
A Capri institution. Good, reliable food.
Author Graham Greene once called this
place his home away from home.

Sfogliatelle

Café Opera

A *salumeria*

Via Madre Serafina 6. Tel: (081) 837 0461. Open: Aug daily noon–3pm, 7.30pm–midnight. Sept–July Tue–Sun noon–3pm, 7.30pm–midnight. Closed mid-Jan–mid-Feb.

Da Tonino**
A family-run find in a quiet rural corner. Meals are strong on tradition, yet always feature a delightful twist. Fish and game dishes are on offer, and the wine cellar is absolutely incredible with over 40,000 bottles to choose from. *Via Dentecale 12. Tel: (081) 837 6718. Open: daily noon–3pm, 7–11pm. Closed mid-Jan–mid-Mar.*

La Capannina****
The most consistently good restaurant in Capri. Come for by-the-book renditions of Capri specialities.

Via Le Botteghe 12 bis. Tel: (081) 837 0732. Open: Apr–Oct daily noon–2pm, 7.30pm–midnight. Mar, Nov Mon, Tue, Thur–Sun noon–2pm, 7.30pm–midnight. Closed mid-Nov–mid-Mar.

La Savardina da Edoardo*
Game and pasta dishes galore at this converted farmhouse/restaurant. Makes a nice change from the usual fish. *Via Lo Capo 8. Tel: (081) 837 6300. Open: July, Aug daily noon–3pm, 7–11pm. Jan, Mar–June, Sept, Oct, Dec Mon, Wed–Sun noon–3pm, 7–11pm. Closed Nov–22 Dec & 7 Jan–Feb.*

Ischia
Alberto a Mare**
Imaginative takes on local favourites, served on a serene blue platform by the sapphire sea.

Via Cristoforo Colombo 8. Tel: (081) 981 259. Open: daily noon–3pm, 7–11pm. Closed Nov–mid-Mar.

Cocò*

A local haunt packed with well-priced pasta and fish dishes.
Piazzale Aragonese. Tel: (081) 981 823. Open: Mar, Apr, Oct–Dec Mon, Tue, Thur–Sun 12.30–3pm, 7.30–11pm. May–Sept daily 12.30–3pm, 7.30–11pm. Closed Jan & Feb.

Damiano***

Considered one of Ischia's top restaurants, standards have recently gone down. The views, and the freshness of its fish dishes, however, keep it near the top of the league tables.
Via Variente Esterna SS270. Tel: (081) 983 032. Open: Mon–Sat 8pm–midnight; Sun noon–3pm, 8pm–midnight. Closed Nov–Mar.

Positano
Il Capitano***

Positano's finest eatery cooks up a wealth of local dishes. Competent and classic is the name of the game.
Via Pasitea 119. Tel: (089) 811 351. Open: Mon, Tue, Thur–Sun noon–3pm, 7.30–10.30pm; Wed 7.30–10.30pm. Closed Nov–Mar.

Il Ritrovo**

A rustic restaurant boasting a fine wooden terrace with views down the valley to the sea. The vegetable antipasti are excellent.
Via Montepertuso 77. Tel: (089) 812 005. Open: May–Oct daily 12.30–3pm, 7pm–midnight. Feb–Apr, Nov, Dec Mon, Tue,

The best local produce

Thur–Sun 12.30–3pm, 7pm–midnight. Closed Jan & 1 week in Feb.

'O Guarracino**

Location, location, location is what makes this restaurant so special. Enjoy the scenic veranda near the cliffs overlooking Fornillo beach.
Via Positanesi d'America 12. Tel: (089) 875 794. Open: mid-June–Sept daily 12.30–3pm, 7pm–midnight. Apr–mid-June, Oct Mon, Wed–Sun 12.30–3pm, 7pm–midnight. Closed Nov–Mar.

Procida
L'Approdo**

Enormous portions of incredible pasta, excellent pizza, and fish so fresh it may still wriggle when it is dished up in front of you.
Via Roma 76. Tel: (081) 896 9930. Open: daily noon–3.30pm, 7.30pm–midnight.

La Conchiglia**

An incredibly romantic, family-run eatery on Chiaja beach. A boat ride is necessary to take you to the intimate tables. And the food is certainly no let-down. Dig in to incredible antipasti, pasta, local fish and fresh veggies.
Access from steps at Via Pizzaco 10, Piazza Olmo. Tel: (081) 896 7602. Open: by appointment. Closed mid-Nov–Mar.

Sorrento
Da Emilia*

An unassuming little restaurant with wooden tables and checked tablecloths. Old-style food, service and people-watching make it an essential stop.

Via Marina Grande 62. Tel: (081) 807 2720. Open: July, Aug daily 12.30–3pm, 7.30–11pm. Apr–June, Sept, Oct Mon, Wed–Sun 12.30–3pm, 7.30–11pm. Nov–Mar subject to weather conditions.

Il Buco***

Situated in the converted cellars of an old convent, *Il Buco* dishes up *nouvelle* Italian cuisine. Portions look small but are surprisingly filling and impeccably well presented.
Seconda Rampa, Marina Piccola 5. Tel: (081) 878 2354. Open: Mon, Tue, Thur–Sun noon–3pm, 7pm–midnight. Closed Jan.

Local 'Tears of Christ' wine

LIMONCELLO

About a hundred years ago, a *Caprese* vintner decided that something had to be done about the island's abundance of lemons. The result: *limoncello*. Today, this sweet lemon-flavoured liqueur is Campania's favourite post-meal *aperitif* and holiday souvenir. While you can buy the stuff on almost every street corner in the region, die-hards will often insist on purchasing it at its source on the island of Capri. **Limoncello di Capri** (*see p151*) is the ancestral home of the luscious lemony liqueur, but producers in Amalfi and Sorrento also whip up some delightful concoctions – even if the bottles they offer differ from the original recipe.

Ristorante Vittoria***

The ultimate Grand Tour dining experience. White-jacketed waiters and silver service. It's all here and more.

Grand Hotel Excelsior, Piazza Tasso 34. Tel: (081) 807 1044. Open: daily 12.30–2pm, 7.30–10pm.

Sant'Antonino**

Basic trattoria serving better-than-average hearty food. Try to visit when the fish barbecue is on offer on the terrace under the orange trees.

Via Santa Maria delle Grazie 6. Tel: (081) 877 1200. Open: May–Oct daily noon–3pm, 7–11.30pm. Dec–Apr Tue–Sun noon–3pm, 7–10.30pm. Closed Nov.

YOUR FRIENDLY, NEIGHBOURHOOD ACQUAFRESCAI

In the days when a drink of Neapolitan water could lead to something more than your thirst being quenched, a distinctly local business was developed to help soothe the stomachs of Campania's anxious residents. *Acquafrescai* (fresh-water sellers) may no longer be required now that the threat of cholera has dwindled, but the tradition lives on. On hot summer days, stallholders sell gallons of their natural drinks. Especially loved is the fizzing *spremuta di limone*, a cocktail of fresh lemons, carbonated spring water and bicarbonate of soda. For a true Neapolitan experience, head over to the brass counter in Piazza Teodoro Monticelli and gulp your way to contentedness.

I scream for ice cream!

The chefs of Naples claim that this delicious delicacy, now ubiquitous throughout the world, was born in the wood-fired ovens of this very city. As such, the status of the dish has been elevated to an art form. Locals will cling to their favourite *pizzerie* with a passion almost as strong as their support for the local football team.

Once a meal for only the poorest of the city, the Neapolitan pizza is now enjoyed by all. In this city you will only find one kind of crust available: thin, crisp and dry: a far cry from the thick, doughy types found in most North American cities.

Many of Naples' best *pizze* are made in rustic locations where staff speak not a word of English and have never heard of a reservation. Don't even think about ordering pineapple on your pizza in a place like this. It will most likely cause many a jaw to drop and a hell of a lot of hysterical laughing. Don't be put off by queues: these places turn over their customers at a remarkably fast rate. To place your order, make your presence known to the head waiter or you may be standing there all night. You can ask for just about any combination of pizza toppings you like, but most locals opt for the *margherita*. Traditional pizzas include:

Caprese: Fresh cherry tomatoes and mozzarella. A few leaves of *rucola* or *rughetta* (rocket) are optional.

Capricciosa: Tomato, black olives, artichokes and ham.

Margherita: Tomato, mozzarella, basil and oil.

Marinara: Tomato, oregano, garlic and oil.

Prosciutto crudo e rucola in bianco: Parma ham, mozzarella and fresh rocket.

Ripieno: A pizza folded pastry-style, stuffed with mozzarella, ricotta and salami and topped with tomato and basil.

Ripieno fritto: A deep-fried version of the above, often containing pieces of pig fat in the filling.

Salsiccia e friarielli: Mozzarella, sausage and *friarielli* (a form of local spinach).

Some of the better *pizzerie* to try out include:

Brandi

The place that claims to have invented the Margherita. Ex-US President Bill Clinton is a former patron.

Salita Sant'Anna di Palazzo 1. Tel: (081) 416 928. Open: daily 12.30–3.30pm, 7pm–midnight.

Da Michele

Minimalist eatery offering only two types of pizza, made perfectly: the *margherita* and *marinara*.

Via Sersale 1. Tel: (081) 553 9204. Open: Mon–Sat 10am–11pm. Closed 2 weeks in Aug.

Di Matteo

High on function and low on form, the pizzas are superb. The décor, however, leaves a lot to be desired.

Via dei Tribunali 94. Tel: (081) 455 262. Open: Mon–Sat 10am–midnight. Closed 2 weeks in Aug.

Lombardi a Santa Chiara

One of the most popular places for a bite in Naples. The selection of sweets and pastries is also quite superb.

Via B Croce 59. Tel: (081) 552 0780. Open: Tue–Sun 1–3pm, 8–11.30pm. Closed 3 weeks in Aug.

Pizzeria Cilea

Great pizza and *frittura* at great prices. Be prepared to queue.

Via Cilea 43. Tel: (081) 556 3291. Open: Mon–Sat 1–4pm, 7–11.30pm; Sun 7.30–11.30pm. Closed 2 weeks in Aug.

Trianon da Ciro

No-frills pizzeria, but all of the offerings are delicious. You may have to write your own order during peak times.

Via Colletta 46. Tel: (081) 553 9426. Open: daily 10.30am–3.30pm, 6.30–11.30pm.

Opposite and above: Naples, home of the pizza
Below: You'll be spoilt for choice with most menus

Hotels and Accommodation

The Italian State Tourist Board operates a star classification system for hotels. The most luxurious is classified as a five-star (*****), while a comfortable, simple *pensione* is classified as a one-star (*). There are no five-star properties in the city of Naples, even though its four-star hotels are often jaw-droppingly luxurious.

Excelsior

During high season from June to September, at Christmas and New Year, hotels are often booked months, if not years, in advance – especially on weekends. This is specially the case for properties in Capri, Ischia and along the Amalfi Coast. Another busy time is during the period of Maggio dei Monumeni, when visitors flock to the city to visit churches, historical sites and private chapels that are usually closed to the general public and local hotel owners raise their prices accordingly.

If you're on a budget, Naples has plenty of options to choose from. Most low-cost hotels stick close to the decidedly unsavoury Piazza Garibaldi. Standards vary widely, so be sure to check your room before you sign the dotted line. In Capri, Ischia, Procida and along the Amalfi Coast, budget options are decidedly thin on the ground. Prices usually start at about €100 for a single bed per night and go up, up and away. Surprisingly, even these outrageously priced properties fill well in advance during high season. Book ahead if you are planning an overnight stay.

If you decide to use the services of a hotel booking agency, be advised that there are no services on offer through any government-sponsored tourist boards. All booking agencies are privately owned and profit-minded, and you will most certainly pay for the ease and convenience.

For a list of each area's hotels, try contacting the local Associazione Albergatori (hoteliers' association) through their website *www.campaniahotels.com*. Otherwise, if you find yourself stranded at the airport with no bed for the night, then give Prom Hotels (*Airport location. Tel: (081) 789 6716. Fax (081) 789 6717. www.girandonapoli.it*) a whirl. A second location at Stazione Centrale is available if you arrive in town by train. Alternatively, just contact any of the hotels listed below directly.

Naples
Luxury hotels
Four-star properties in Naples include: **Britannique****** *Corso Vittorio Emanuele 133. Tel: (081) 761 4145. www.hotelbritannique.it*

Caravaggio**** *Piazza Riario Sforza 157. Tel: (081) 211 0066. www.caravaggiohotel.it*
Excelsior**** *Via Partenope 48. Tel: (081) 764 0111. www.excelsior.it*
Grand Hotel Parker's**** *Corso Vittorio Emanuele 135. Tel: (081) 761 2474. www.grandhotelparkers.com*
Holiday Inn**** *Via Centro Direzionale, Isola E6. Tel: (081) 225 0111. www.hotel-invest.com*
Hotel San Francesco al Monte**** *Corso Vittorio Emanuele 328. Tel: (081) 251 2461. www.hotelsanfrancesco.it*
Majestic**** *Largo Vasto a Chiaia 68. Tel: (081) 416 500. www.majestic.it*
Miramare**** *Via Depretis 123. Tel: (081) 552 9500. www.accorhotel.com*
Paradiso**** *Via Catullo 11. Tel: (081) 761 4161. www.bestwestern.it*
Santa Lucia**** *Via Partenope 46. Tel: (081) 764 0666. www.santalucia.it*
Vesuvio**** *Via Partenope 45. Tel: (081) 764 0044. www.vesuvio.it*

Budget hotels
Some of the more affordable hotels are:
Canada*** *Via Mergellina 43. Tel: (081) 680 952. www.sea-hotels.com*
Chiaia Hotel de Charme*** *Via Chiaia 216. Tel: (081) 415 555. www.hotelchiaia.it*

Foyer at Grand Hotel Parker's

Crispi* *Via F Crispi. Tel: (081) 668 048.*
Hotel Cavour*** *Piazza Garibaldi 32. Tel: (081) 283 122. www.hotelcavournapoli.it*
Le Fontane al Mare* *Via N Tommaseo 14. Tel: (081) 764 3811.*
Parteno*** *Via Partenope 1. Tel: (081) 245 2095. www.parteno.it*
Pinto-Storey** *Via G Martucci 72. Tel: (081) 681 260. www.pintostorey.it*
Ruggiero* *Via Martucci 72. Tel: (081) 663 536.*
Toledo*** *Via Montecalvario 15. Tel: (081) 406 871. www.sea-hotels.com/www.hoteltoledo.com*

Hostels
Surprisingly, hostels aren't really a popular option in the area. Two options to consider include:
Agriturismo Il Casolare di Tobia *Contrada Coast di Baia, Via Selvatico 12, Bacoli. Tel: (081) 523 5193. Please note that this hostel is located in a farmhouse outside of the city centre.*
Ostello Mergellina (Youth Hostel) *Salita della Grotta a Piedigrotta 23. Tel: (081) 761 2346/(081) 761 1215.*

Private homes
Try the following service if you prefer to rent an apartment or just a room in a private home. You will be given a choice of properties before you pay.
Rent a Bed *Vico Sergente Maggiore 16. Tel: (081) 417 721. www.rentabed.com*

Camping
Two registered campsites are located in nearby Pozzuoli, but neither is within easy reach of the city centre. They're close to the sea, but not really convenient for anywhere else. Both are

Doorman at the Excelsior, Naples

situated in rustically beautiful spots in the western tip of Naples.

Averno *Via Montenuovo Licola Patria 85, Arco Felice Lucrino, Pozzuoli. Tel: (081) 804 2666.*

Vulcano Solfatara *Via Solfatara 161, Pozzuoli. Tel: (081) 526 7413. www.solfatara.it*

Amalfi

Elegant hotels make up the bulk of what's on offer in Amalfi, including two converted from old monasteries. No longer quite as austere, properties tend to be family-run and impeccable.

Cappuccini Convento**** *Via Annunziatella 46. Tel: (089) 871 877. www.amalfinet.it/cappuccini*

La Bussola**** *Lungomare dei Cavalieri 1. Tel: (089) 871 533. Email: labussola@amalficoast.it*

Luna Torre Saracena**** *Via Comite 33. Tel: (089) 871 002. www.lunahotel.it*

Santa Caterina***** *Strada Statale Amalfitana 9. Tel: (089) 871 012. www.santacaterina.it*

Capri

Prepare to take out a second mortgage if you are looking to stay on Capri in high season. Prices are deliberately

inflated in order to encourage a higher class of tourist. Many hotels close from November to mid-March, with limited opening during the Christmas period. Book in advance to avoid disappointment.

Belvedere e Tre Re*** *Via Marina Grande 138. Tel: (081) 837 0345. www.belvedere-tre-re.com*

Gatto Bianco**** *Via Vittorio Emanuele 32. Tel: (081) 837 0203.*

La Palma**** *Via Vittorio Emanuele 39. Tel: (081) 837 0133. www.lapalma-capri.com*

La Tosca* *Via Birago 5. Tel: (081) 837 0989. Email: h.tosca@capri.it*

Quisisana***** *Via Camerelle 2. Tel: (081) 837 0788. www.quisi.com*

San Michele*** *Via G Orlandi. Tel: (081) 837 1442. Email: smichele@capri.it*

Villa Brunella***** *Via Tregara 24a. Tel: (081) 837 0122. www.villabrunella.it*

Villa Krupp**** *Via G Matteotti 12. Tel: (081) 837 0362.*

Ischia

Ischia rivals Capri in hotel quality and price. Once again, high season is busy and beds are like gold dust. Book ahead.

Casa Conchiglia** *Via Chiaia delle Rose 3. Tel: (081) 999 270.*

Hotel della Baia*** *Via San Montano 18/22. Tel: (081) 986 342. www.negombo.it*

Hotel Regina Isabella***** *Piazza Santa Restituta. Tel: (081) 994 322. www.reginaisabella.it*

Il Monastero** *Castello Aragonese. Tel: (081) 992 435. www.castelloaragonese.it*

Il Moresco Grand Hotel e Terme**** *Via E Gianturco 16. Tel: (081) 981 355. www.ilmoresco.it*

Il Vitigno** *Via Bocca 31.*
Tel: (081) 998 307.
La Villarosa**** *Via G Gigante 5. Tel:*
(081) 991 316. Email: hotel@villarosa.it
Mezzatorre***** *Località San Montano.*
Tel: (081) 986 111.
Email: info@mezzatorre.it
Miramare e Castello***** *Via Pontano*
9. Tel: (081) 991 333.
Email: mircastl@metis.it
Park Hotel Miramare***** *Via*
Comandante Maddalena 29.
Tel: (081) 999 219. www.hotelmiramare.it

Positano

Positano has plenty of hotels to choose
from, with many built for function
rather than form. Converted villas
and 18th-century residences, while
expensive, are your best bet.
Casa Albertina*** *Via della Tavolozza 3.*
Tel: (089) 875 143. Email: alcaal@starnet.it
Casa Soriano** *Via Pasitea 108.*
Tel: (089) 875 494.
Le Sireneuse***** *Via C Colombo 30.*
Tel: (089) 875 066.
Palazzo Murat***** *Via dei Mulini 23.*
Tel: (089) 875 177.

Jolly Hotel, Naples

Poseidon**** *Via Pasitea 148. Tel: (089)*
811 111.www.hotelposeidonpositano.it
San Pietro***** *Via Laurito 2. Tel:*
(089) 875 455. www.ilsanpietro.it

Procida

Procida's small size is reflected in its
smaller hotel options. The best bets are
intimate, family-run *pensiones* in the
fishermen's quarter. Two options are:
Crescenzo** *Marina della Chiaiolella.*
Tel: (081) 896 7255.
Pensione Gentile** *Marina Corricella.*
Tel: (081) 896 7799.

Ravello

Ravello has a number of charming
family-run hotels, all with colourful
histories. Prices match their status as
historical landmarks.
Caruso Belvedere*** *Piazza San*
Giovanni del Toro 2. Tel: (089) 857 111.
Graal**** *Via della Repubblica 4.*
Tel: (089) 857 222. www.hotelgraal.it
Palumbo**** *Via San Giovanni del*
Toro 28. Tel: (089) 857 244.
www.hotelpalumbo.it
Villa Cimbrone***** *Via Santa Chiara*
26. Tel: (089) 857 459.
www.villacimbrone.it

Sorrento

Bellevue Syrene***** *Piazza della*
Vittoria 5. Tel: (081) 878 1024.
www.bellevue.it
Excelsior Vittoria***** *Piazza Tasso 34.*
Tel: (081) 807 1044.
Email: exvitt@exvitt.it
Imperial Tramontano***** *Via Veneto 1.*
Tel: (081) 878 2588. www.tramontano.it
Loreley et Londres** *Via Califano 2.*
Tel: (081) 807 3187.

On Business

Naples is the largest major city in southern Italy. Doing business here can be a bit of a chore – in this town the meaning of the words 'I need it right now' tends to fall on deaf ears. Long lunches and extended weekends are perfectly acceptable: after all, if you lived here, wouldn't you want to enjoy the great outdoors?

Holiday Inn

The Italian government has done much in the past few years to spark the economy into overdrive, and during the mid-1990s, Naples was Italy's symbol of regeneration and growth. Things have slowed down a bit now, but there are efforts to turn parts of the city into a tax-free business zone. As with everything involving government in Naples, things are progressing slowly.

Business hours
Most businesses open Monday–Friday 9am–6pm. Retail shops stay open until 8pm with a 2- to 3-hour lunch break starting around 1.30pm. Many companies close for the entire month of August. Banks open Monday–Friday 8.20am–1.20pm, 2.45–3.45pm.

Conference centres
Most of the major Naples hotels have conference facilities. Of particular note is the Holiday Inn, located in the big business district of Centro Direzionale. If you would rather go through a conference-organising company, there aren't that many to choose from. The following will smooth the way by helping you select a location, and they will completely organise all the details for you.

GP Relazioni Pubbliche
Via San Pasquale a Chiaia 55, Chiaia.
Tel: (081) 401 201.
Email: gpcongress@napoli.com

Couriers
Local and international couriers include **DHL** (*tel: 199 199 345*), **Fedex** (*tel: 800 123 800*), **Freccia Azzurra** (*tel: (081) 552 1520*), **Tartaruga Service** (*tel: (081) 202 027*), **TNT** (*tel: 800 803 868*) and **UPS** (*tel: 800 877 877*).

Etiquette
If you are meeting business clients in Naples you should dress smartly – men should wear a suit, since it is best to assume that formal wear is what is required. Don't be surprised if your colleague turns up extremely late: in Naples this is standard practice and not a sign of rudeness. Usually, it is due to the horrific traffic that plagues the city. Don't take being late as the general rule of thumb, though: as the foreign guest, you are advised to turn up right on time.

Internet access and cafés

You can get Internet access at various points throughout the city.

Clic Net
Via Toledo 393, Toledo. Tel: (081) 552 9370. Open: Mon–Sat 9.30am–9.30pm.

Internet Bar
Piazza Bellini, Centro Storico. Tel: (081) 295 237. Open: Mon–Sat 9am–2am, Sun 8pm–2am.

Multimedia Napoli
Via Sapienza 43, Centro Storico. Tel: (081) 298 412. Open: daily 9.30am–9.30pm.

Interpreters

Outfits include:

AIT Coop
Via Depretis 88, Port & University. Tel: (081) 551 3507.

GIC'90
Via Monte di Dio 66, Royal. Tel: (081) 764 7427.

Office services and supplies

There are stationery and computer shops dotted throughout the city centre, and you should be able to get any materials you require on your trip.

Mail Boxes, etc.
Via Bracco 57/59, Port & University. Tel: (081) 580 0256. Open: 9.30am–6.30pm.

Relocation

To live and work in Naples, you will need to be an EU citizen. You must bring proof to the police that you can support yourself, or that you're in full-time education, in order to get a *permesso di soggiorno* (permit to stay).

Caruso's piano at the Vesuvio, Naples

Practical Guide

Arriving
Formalities

Visitors to Italy who are citizens of the UK, Ireland, Australia, the US, Canada or New Zealand will need a passport, but not a visa for stays of up to three months. After that time, they must apply for a *permesso di soggiorno* (permit to stay). If you are travelling from other countries, you may need a visa, and it is best to check before you leave home.

By air

Capodichino Airport (*tel: (081) 751 5371. www.gesac.it*) is southern Italy's largest international airport and it is about 8km (5 miles) from the Stazione Centrale rail station. There are a number of ways to get from the airport into the centre of town.

CLP: Connects to Piazza Garibaldi in front of the Stazione Centrale and Piazza Municipio (near the ferry port) via blue buses that depart from outside the airport's arrivals lounge.
Tel: (081) 5311 706. Departs every 40 minutes. Operates 6am–11pm daily. www.clpbus.com

By public bus: Local orange bus number 3S runs from outside the arrivals lounge to Piazza Garibaldi and the ferry port. *Departs every 5 minutes when landings are scheduled.*

By taxi: A fare from the airport to central Naples should cost €15–€20. There is a surcharge of €2.58 for all airport runs.

To Sorrento and the Sorrentine Peninsula: Autolinee Curreri ((*081) 801 5420)* runs six buses daily from outside arrivals. Tickets: €5.20.

By rail

You will most likely arrive at the Stazione Centrale in the heart of Naples on the Piazza Garibaldi. Some late-night long-distance rail services terminate at Stazione Campi Flegrei in the eastern suburbs.

By sea

The ports nearest to Naples are Molo Beverello, Mergellina and Pozzuoli.

Molo Beverello: Naples' premier ferry and hydrofoil port. Arrivals and departures to/from Capri, Ischia, Procida, Sorrento and the Amalfi Coast. Mediterranean cruise-liners also disembark from the city-centre dock.

Mergellina: Hydrofoil services to and from Capri, Ischia and Procida.

Pozzuoli: Car ferries for Procida and Ischia. The port is located 12km (8 miles) northwest of Naples.

Cars and driving
Breakdown

The **ACI** (*tel: (081) 239 4511*) and **Touring Club Italia** (*tel: (081) 420 3485*) offer breakdown services.

Car hire

Most car-hire companies will have offices at the airport. The majority of their cars will be manual, but there are a limited number of automatic cars for hire. To get the best deal and guarantee availability, book a car before you leave home. Booking on the Internet can give considerable savings. To rent a car in Italy you must be over 21 (25 to rent a larger-cylinder car) and be able to produce a full valid driving licence from your country of residence. The usual hire rate quoted will cover third party/liability insurance, unlimited mileage, VAT and passenger indemnity insurance. It is recommended that you take out the additional collision damage waiver, so that you are not liable for replacement of the car. If you have an accident or the car breaks down, inform the car-hire company immediately.

Driving

Nothing can prepare you for the sheer volume of cars on the streets of the city. Avoid the rush-hour traffic, which is at its worst during wet weather and on Fridays. Don't drink and drive.

Fuel

There are few petrol stations in the centre of Naples. In every petrol station there are usually unleaded, leaded and diesel pumps. Credit card facilities are hit-and-miss.

Parking

Finding parking in Naples is virtually impossible. If you do find a space, you will need to purchase a pay-and-display ticket, scratch card or parking debit card from a street-side dispensing machine,

An authorised taxi

tabacchi, or *edicole* (newsstand). Look for blue lines on the road to ensure that your space is permitted. The streets are patrolled by traffic wardens who issue tickets liberally for transgressors. Illegal parking attendants operate in many areas: they will claim to 'look after' your car for about €1. The safest option is to use a pay car park, especially if you need to leave your car overnight and/or have foreign registration. If you do park illegally your car will be clamped and/or you will pay a fine, or it might be towed away and you will have to pay to remove it from the pound.

In the event that you do find a space on the road that isn't marked with a blue line, go ahead and park – with three exceptions. Look for signs saying *passo carrabile* (access at all times), *sosta vietata* (no parking) and disabled parking spaces marked with yellow lines. The sign *zona rimozione* (tow-away area) means no parking and is valid until the end of the street, or until the next tow-away sign with a red line through it.

Via Brin (*Via B Brin, tel: (081) 763 2855*) runs an 850-car facility between the Stazione Centrale and the port. Find it by taking the Porto exit from the ring road or motorway. Shuttle buses leave for the ferry port at Molo Beverello every 10 minutes.

Traffic regulations

Drive on the right and use a seatbelt. Always carry your driving licence with you. The law states that you need to carry a hazard triangle in your car at all times, and remember the following tips to avoid an accident:

- Flashing your lights means that you will **not** slow down or give way.

- Locals often ignore red lights, so approach any junction with caution. If traffic lights flash amber, stop and give way to the right.
- Watch out for scooters and pedestrians. Both will fully expect you to stop if they decide to move in front of you.

For traffic updates, phone 166 664 477 for 24-hour information with English-speaking operators. Cars are forbidden on the island of Capri.

Crime

Crime has always been a big problem for the city of Naples. Its reputation is actually far worse than reality. Petty theft (bag-snatching, pickpocketing) is the most common form of trouble for tourists, and activity is particularly high in the much-frequented historic sites. You are unlikely to experience violence or assault, which occur mainly in the context of gangland activities.

Don't carry too much cash and avoid walking around alone very late at night on badly lit streets (especially if you are a woman). Your hotel will warn you about particular areas to avoid.

Attitude is everything. Look as if you know what you're doing and where you're going. Do not carry your wallet in your back pocket, especially on buses. Keep your bags closed with your hand on them at all times, and do not leave your bag or coat on the ground where you cannot see them. When walking down the street, be sure to wear camera straps and bags crossed over your chest. Make sure the bag and/or camera is on the side away from the street so as to prevent robberies from motorbike thieves. And whatever you do, stay away from cute children.

Often, they are employed as part of larger gangs and are masters at removing your most precious items.

Car theft is also a problem. Do not leave valuables in an unattended rental car (they can recognise the registration) or in a car with foreign registration.

Customs regulations

Duty-free goods are only available to those who visit Italy from outside the EU. You can also purchase duty-free goods if you are flying directly from Italy to a non-EU country, or if you fly to a non-EU country via an EU country stopover (but you must leave the EU on the same day). If you have come from outside the EU you are allowed 200 cigarettes, 2 litres of wine and 1 litre of spirits. Particular emphasis is placed on the ban on importing foodstuff, particularly meat products in the light of recent outbreaks of foot and mouth disease and BSE.

Electricity

The standard electrical current is 220 volts. Two-pin adaptor plugs can be purchased at most electrical shops.

Embassies and consulates

American Consulate Piazza della Repubblica, Mergellina. *Tel: (081) 583 8111.*

British Consulate Via dei Mille 40, Chiaia. *Tel: (081) 423 8911.*

Canadian Consulate Via G Carducci 29, Chiaia. *Tel: (081) 401 338.*

Australians and New Zealanders requiring diplomatic assistance should consult their embassies in Rome.

Emergency telephone numbers

The emergency telephone numbers in Italy are 113 and 112 (police), 115 (fire), 118 (ambulance), 803 116 (car breakdown), 1530 (coastguard) and 151 (forest rangers and mountain rescue).

Entertainment guides

The Naples Tourist Board produces a 'what's on' booklet, *Qui Napoli*, which lists cultural events, exhibitions and transport timetables. The national newspapers also provide listings of events throughout the city and beyond – in Italian only.

Look out for *Le Pagine dell'Ozio* and *Leggo, City* for current art and entertainment listings.

Health

Visitors from the EU are entitled to free treatment under the EU Reciprocal Medical Treatment Programme. You should collect an E111 form before you travel. If you need to see a doctor, tell the office that you want to be treated under EU social security arrangements. Visitors from countries outside the EU should ensure that they have adequate insurance cover before they leave their country of origin. In an emergency, go to the *Pronto Soccorso* (casualty) department of one of the major hospitals.

In Naples:
Cardarelli (*Via Cardarelli 9. Tel: (081) 747 1111*), Santobono (*Via M Fiore 6. Tel: (081) 220 5797*).

On Capri:
Ospedale Capilupi (*Via Provinciale Anacapri. Tel: (081) 838 1205*).

On Ischia:
Ospedale Anna Rizzoli (*Via Fundara. Tel: (081) 507 9267*).

In Sorrento:
Ospedale Civico (*Corso Italia. Tel: (081) 533 1111*).

Hiring a bike or scooter

Riding a bike is one of the best ways to see Naples, but be sure to wear a helmet at all times. If you need to hire a scooter, try one of the car rental agencies. For a bike try Napoli Bike (*Riviera di Chiaia 201. Tel: (081) 411 934*).

Insurance

You should take out personal travel insurance from your travel agent, tour operator or insurance company. It should give adequate cover for medical expenses, loss or theft, repatriation, personal liability, third-party motor insurance (but liability arising from motor accidents is not usually included) and cancellation expenses. If you hire a car, collision insurance (often called collision damage waiver or CDW) is usually compulsory and charged by the hirer, but it may be as much as 50 per cent of the hiring fee. Check with your own motor insurers before you leave, as you may already be covered for CDW on overseas hires by your normal policy.

Neither CDW nor your personal travel insurance will protect you from liability arising from an accident in a hire car – for example, if you damage another vehicle or injure someone. If you are likely to hire a car you should obtain some extra cover, preferably from your travel agent or other insurer before departure. If you take your own motor vehicle on holiday, check with your motor insurers on your cover for damage, loss or theft of the vehicle and for liability. A Green Card (third-party cover) is recommended for those from European countries outside the EU. The Green Card can be obtained from your local motor insurer, but it is not required for visitors coming from another EU country.

Lost property

If you lose an important personal item or it is stolen, inform the *polizia* or *carabinieri* (police) straight away. They will fill out a report and you can then claim the value of the loss from your insurance company.

Maps

The Osservatorio Turistico-Culturale on the Piazza del Plebiscito has probably the best selection of free maps of the city centre. When in other towns in the region, head to the local tourist office. Newsstands, *tabacchi*, ports and tourist sites always have maps available for sale.

Media

The Italian media are well established and there are some excellent (if slightly tacky and outrageous) home-produced programmes on local television and radio. English-language broadcasting is almost non-existent, but most hotels will have satellite TV in the bedrooms. There are more than a few local radio stations, and talk radio and football programming are very popular in Italy.

The major national daily newspapers fall strictly along political lines. While they may look national in scope, most Italian papers are strictly regional. The largest

daily in the city is *Il Mattino*; however, the Rome-based daily *La Repubblica* and Milan's *Corriere della Sera* both have Neapolitan sections. Sports coverage in the dailies is generally extensive – especially when covering national football results. Three sports-specific rags to try out include *Corriere dello Sport, La Gazzetta dello Sport* and *Tuttosport*. None of the above publications offer English-language sections. To keep up to date you can usually buy European versions of the British press and the *International Herald Tribune*.

Money matters

The currency in Italy is the euro. If you are coming from another country in the EU (with the euro currency) you will not need to change money. A euro is divided into 100 cents. The currency denominations are: 50 euro, 20 euro, 10 euro, 5 euro, 2 euro, 1 euro, 50 cents, 20 cents, 10 cents, 5 cents and 1 cent. You can withdraw money using ATM at many Italian banks.

Changing money

Thomas Cook has an exchange bureau at the airport, open daily from 5.30am–9.30pm (departures) or 8am–10.30pm (arrivals). Foreign exchange counters of major banks also change money.

Traveller's cheques are a safe way to carry large amounts of money when you are on holiday. Thomas Cook provides an excellent Traveller's Cheques service and offers a 24-hour refund service if they are lost or stolen (*tel: 0044 1733 319 8950 and reverse the charges*).

Credit cards

All major credit cards are accepted at most hotels, restaurants and shops in

Policemen are friendly and helpful

Naples. You may not be so lucky at smaller establishments. If you lose your credit card or it is stolen, inform your credit card company straight away.

Pharmacies

There are plenty of pharmacies (called *farmacia*, identified by a large red or green cross) in the city centre. Most Italian pharmacists are highly qualified and give good advice on minor ailments and first aid, and they also provide a range of over-the-counter drugs without a prescription. Chemists in the city centre with Saturday openings (rare in Naples) and who speak some English include:

Cristiano *Riviera di Chiaia 77, Chiaia. Tel: (081) 681 544. Open: Mon–Sat 9am–1pm, 4–8pm. Closed Aug.*
Farmacia d'Atri *Piazza Municipio 15, Royal. Tel: (081) 552 4237. Open: Mon–Sat 9am–1pm, 4–8.30pm. Closed Aug.*

Police

The Neapolitan police force is called the *carabinieri*. Officers are very approachable; however, few speak English. They are friendly and helpful and usually happy to help tourists with directions or any other information you require. The nearest police station to the city centre is the *Questura Centrale* (central police station) at Via Medina 75 (*tel: (081) 794 1111*).

Post offices

Usual opening hours for the *Palazzo Centrale della Posta* (central post office) are Mon–Fri 8.15am–7pm, Sat 8.15am–noon. The post office is situated on the Piazza Matteotti.

Public Holidays

The Italian Public Holidays are:

1 January	*Capodanno* (New Year's Day)
6 January	*La Befana* (Epiphany)
Easter Monday	*Pasquetta*
25 April	*Festa della Liberazione* (Liberation Day)
1 May	*Festa del Lavoro* (Labour Day)
15 August	*Ferragosto* (Feast of the Assumption)
1 November	*Tuttisanti* (All Saints' Day)
8 December	*L'Immacolata* (Feast of the Immaculate Conception)
25 December	*Natale* (Christmas Day)
26 December	*Santo Stefano* (Boxing Day)

Naples and the surrounding area also shuts down on **19 September**, the feast of the city's patron saint, San Gennaro.

LANGUAGE

Naples may be in Italy, but the dialect is unlike that of any other part of the country. Few people speak English except in Sorrento, which is popular with British holidaymakers. Here is a list of Italian words and phrases with their English translations. Terms in italics are local colloquialisms and shouldn't be used outside Campania:

Afternoon	pomeriggio
Evening	sera
Night	notte
Weekend	fine settimana, *weekend*
Hello/Goodbye	(informal) ciao
Hello	(informal) salve
Good morning	buon giorno
Good evening	buona sera
Goodnight	buona notte
Please	per favore, per piacere
Thank you	grazie
You're welcome	prego
Excuse me, sorry	mi scusi (formal), scusa (informal), *shcusate* (formal and informal)
I'm sorry	mi dispiace, *dishpiasher*
I don't speak Italian	non parlo l'italiano, *non parl' buon' l'italian'*
I don't/didn't understand	non capisco, non ho capito, *n'aggio capit'*
How much is (it)?	quando costa?, quando viene?
Open	aperto, *apierto*
Closed	chiuso
Entrance	entrata
Exit	uscita
Where is?	Dov'e?, *a ro'sta?*

COMMUNICATIONS

Phone	telefono
Email	posta elettronica
Fax	fax
Stamp/s	francobollo/i
Letter	lettera
Postcard	cartolina

DAYS AND NIGHTS

Monday	lunedì
Tuesday	martedì
Wednesday	mercoledì
Thursday	giovedì
Friday	venerdì, *viernari*
Saturday	sabato
Sunday	domenica, *rumenica*
Today	oggi
Tomorrow	domain, *rimane*
Morning	mattina
See you tomorrow	a domani

NUMBERS

0	zero	**7**	sette
1	uno	**8**	otto
2	due	**9**	nove
3	tre	**10**	dieci
4	quattro	**20**	venti
5	cinque	**50**	cinquanta
6	sei	**100**	cento

TRANSPORT

Bus	autobus
Coach	pullman
Train	treno
Underground railway	metropolitana (metro)
Platform	binario
Ticket/s	biglietto/i
A ticket for...	un biglietto per...
One way	sola andata
Return	andata e ritorno
Right	destra
Left	sinistra

EAT, SHOP, SLEEP

Reservation, booking
una prenotazione
I'd like to book a table for four at eight
vorrei prenotare una tavola per quattro
persone alle otto
Breakfast/lunch/dinner
colazione/pranzo/cena
The bill
il conto
Is service included?
è compreso il servizio?

That was poor/good (really) delicious
era mediocre/buono/ (davvero) ottimo
I think there's a mistake in this bill
credo che il conto sia sbagliato
100g/300g/1kg/5kg of...
un etto/tre etti/un kilo (chilo)/cinque chili di
More/less
ancora/di meno
A single/twin/double room
una camera singola/doppia/matrimoniale
A room with a (sea) view
una camera con vista (sul mare)

Public transport

ANM buses: Routes run from 6am until roughly 11.30pm. Last buses leave the main termini of Piazza Garibaldi, Piazza Municipio and on Via Pisanelli. There is a limited nightlink service on some routes. *For further information and a complete guide to the bus service and timetables for individual routes, contact ANM toll-free on 800 639 525/www.anm.it. Open: 8am–6pm.*

Metro: The new metro system is quick, clean and efficient. It's so new, there are only a limited number of stations; more are in development. Two lines service the city centre: Metro Linea 1 (from Piazza Dante to Piazza Vanvitelli and on to the northeastern suburbs) and Metro Linea 2 (from Piazza Garibaldi through the Centro Storico and on to Mergellina). Trains run from 5.38am–11.52pm, depending on the line. *For information call the toll-free info line, tel: 800 568 866.*

Local railways: The two main overground lines you are likely to use are the Ferrovia Cumana and the Ferrovia Circumvesuviana. The Ferrovia Cumana operates services from Piazza Montesanto to Campi Flegrei (5.21am–9.41pm). The Ferrovia Circumvesuviana leaves from its own terminus in Corso Garibaldi, south of the Stazione Centrale. Trains run southeast to Pompeii, Herculaneum and Sorrento (dawn–10.30pm). *For further information, contact the train operators directly. Ferrovia Cumana (tel: (081) 551 3328. www.sepsa.it). Ferrovia Circumvesuviana (tel: (081) 772 2444. www.vesuviana.it).*

Religious worship

The main religion is Roman Catholicism but there are also a few Protestant churches to choose from. Your hotel will provide you with information about Sunday service times.

Senior citizens

There are various discounts available for senior visitors to Naples. Travel is offered at a reduced rate if you are over 65, and you will get into museums and galleries at a reduced rate of admission. You will need identification to prove your age.

Student and youth travel

If you are under 18 you are entitled to reduced fares when you travel on public transport. You will need to prove your age with an identification card. If you are over 18 and a student, you will need a student card (for example, the International Student Identity Card) to claim discounts.

Taxis

Taxis can be hailed on the street or at special taxi ranks. Three of the major ranks are at the Piazza Garibaldi, Piazza Dante and Piazza Municipio. The best way to get a taxi is to phone for one: your hotel or restaurant should do this for you. Be sure only to use authorised white taxis emblazoned with the city emblem on the front doors and rear licence plates.

Taxis differ outside Naples. In Capri they are often vintage and/or convertible cars. Sorrento has horse-drawn carriages and Ischia boasts three-wheeled micro-cabs. Fare structures are extremely loose outside Naples; prices should be negotiated with the driver before departing.

Telephone

Telephone numbers in the Naples area have six or seven digits with 081 as the prefix and 39 if you are dialling from abroad. Most phone booths accept phone and/or credit cards: coins are accepted in only a few locations. Instructions for use of the phone are in English. For directory enquiries within Italy, dial 12. For international enquiries, dial 176.

Time

Italy maintains Continental European Time (GMT+1). Clocks go forward one hour in spring and back in autumn, in line with all other EU countries.

Toilets

There are very few public toilet facilities in Naples. The best approach is to use the toilet in a bar: you can usually walk straight in without having to buy a drink. If the bar is empty it is a matter of politeness to ask the bartender first. In restaurants there may be signs saying that toilets are only for use by customers. Fast-food joints and department stores are other good options if you need a rest.

Tourist information

For information about Italy, the main tourist body is the Italian State Tourist Board.

For those who live in the UK, *contact the Italian State Tourist Board, 1 Princes St, London W1B 2AY. Tel: 020 7399 3562. Email: italy@italiantouristboard.co.uk. www.enit.it. In the US, contact Italian Government Tourist Board, 500 North Michigan Avenue, Suite 2240, Chicago, IL 60611. Tel: (312) 644 0996. Email: enitich@italiantourism.com. www.italiantourism.com; or Italian Government Tourism Board, 12400 Wilshire Blvd, Suite 550, Los Angeles, CA 90025. Tel: (310) 820 1898. Email: enitla@italiantourism.com. www.italiantourism.com; or Italian Government Tourist Board, 630 Fifth Ave., Suite 1565, New York, NY 10111. Tel: (212) 245 4822. Email: enitny@italiantourism.com. www.italiantourism.com. In Canada, contact Italian Government Tourist Board, 175 Bloor St E, Suite 907-South Tower,*

*Toronto, Ont. M4W 3R8. Tel: (416) 925
4882. Email: enit.canada@on.aibn.com
www.italiantourism.com. In Australia,
contact Italian Government Tourist Board,
Level 26, 44 Market St, Sydney, NSW
2000. Email: enitour@ihug.com.au
www.enit.it*

For more specific information on
Naples, there are four organisations that
provide comprehensive tourism
information services.

ASST *Via San Carlo 9. Tel: (081) 402 394.
www.inaples.it*

Ente Provinciale del Turismo (EPT)
*Piazza dei Matiri 58. Tel: (081) 405 311.
www.ept.napoli.it*

Hello Napoli *Tel: 800 251 396.
www.hellonapoli.org*

Osservatorio Turistico-Culturale *Piazza
del Plebiscito. Tel: (081) 247 1123.
www.comune.napoli.it*

Travellers with disabilities

For people with disabilities Naples is a
notoriously difficult city to get by in. The
best thing to do is to ask if someone can
help you, as they may have ramps that
can be placed over stairs. In museums
the ground floors are usually accessible,
as are those in the more modern
galleries. Buses, however, are completely
wheelchair unfriendly. If you need to
get around, try using the metro and
overground trains instead. New metro
stations have wheelchair access features
(ramps and lifts) incorporated into
the design. But even where ramps exist,
you will often find them obstructed by
cars or motorcycles. Lifts are often too
small for a wheelchair to enter and the
narrow, cobblestoned streets can
be uncomfortable.

The historic sites of Pompeii and
Herculaneum, while outdoors, are little
better. Access to the actual collection of
ruins may have ramps, but the pathways
date back to the original Roman period
and are littered with wheel ruts and
cracks making manoeuvrability difficult.

Weather

Naples has a Mediterranean climate with
sizzling temperatures and high humidity
in the summer. On the islands and coast,
sea breezes make the heat more bearable.

Spring and autumn are warm and
pleasant with occasional short, heavy
showers. March and October are good
times to visit the islands when the crowds
are gone and you may see freak summer
temperatures. Between November and
February Naples can be bright and
pleasantly warm with occasional spells of
cloudy, dreary weather.

In December and January a dusting
of snow can be seen on top of Vesuvius.
The air is extremely clear, offering
spectacular visibility.

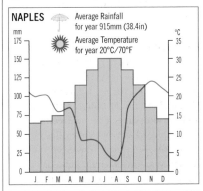

NAPLES Average Rainfall
for year 915mm (38.4in)

Average Temperature
for year 20°C/70°F

Weather Conversion Chart
25.4mm = 1 inch
°F = 1.8 × °C + 32

ents

191

IENTS

hing wishes to thank the photographer, CONOR CAFFREY, for the
iphs reproduced in this book, to whom the copyright in the

Copy-editing: JAN WILTSHIRE

Index: INDEXING SPECIALISTS (UK) LTD

Maps: PC GRAPHICS, Old Woking, UK

Proof-reading: CAMBRIDGE PUBLISHING MANAGEMENT LTD, KEVIN PARNELL
and RICHARD HALL

Travellers

Feedback Form

Please help us improve future editions by taking part in our reader survey. Every returned form will be acknowledged. To show our appreciation we will send you a voucher entitling you to £1 off your next *Travellers* guide or any other Thomas Cook guidebook ordered direct from Thomas Cook Publishing. Just take a few minutes to complete and return this form to us.

We'd also be glad to hear of your comments, updates or recommendations on places we cover or you think that we ought to cover.

1. Which *Travellers* guide did you purchase?

_____

2. Have you purchased other *Travellers* guides in the series?

Yes ☐

No ☐

If Yes, please specify_____

3. Which of the following tempted you into buying your *Travellers* guide:
(Please tick as many as appropriate)

The price ☐

The FREE weblinks CD ☐

The cover ☐

The content ☐

Other_____

4. What do you think of :

a) the cover design? _____

b) the design and layout styles within the book?_____

c) the FREE weblinks CD?_____

5. Please tell us about any features that in your opinion could be changed, improved or added in future editions of the book or CD:

_____

_____

Your age category: ☐ under 21 ☐ 21-30 ☐ 31-40 ☐ 41-50 ☐ 51+

Mr/Mrs/Miss/Ms/Other

Surname_____ Initials_____

Full address: (Please include postal or zip code)_____

_____

Daytime telephone number: _____

Email address: _____

☐ Please tick here if you would be willing to participate in further customer surveys.

☐ Please tick here if you would like to receive information on new titles or special offers from Thomas Cook Publishing (please note we never give your details to third party companies).

Please detach this page and send it to: **The Editor, Travellers, Thomas Cook Publishing, PO Box 227, The Thomas Cook Business Park, Peterborough PE3 8XX, United Kingdom.**

tear along the perforation

The Editor, Travellers
Thomas Cook Publishing
PO Box 227
The Thomas Cook Business Park
Peterborough, PE3 8XX
United Kingdom